BARBARA WATSON

AMAZING HEALTH COOKBOOK

SWEET
SAVORY
SIMPLE

8 INCLUDES
SECRETS
FOR A
LONGER
AND
STRONGER
LIFE!

Copyright © 2012 by Published by Review and Herald® Publishing Association

Published by Review and Herald® Publishing Association, Hagerstown, MD 21741-1119 and
Amazing Facts, Inc., P. O. Box 1058, Roseville, CA 95678-8058

Cover design by Bryan Gray / Review & Herald Design Center
Principal Photography by René Paille

16 15 14 13 12   5 4 3 2 1

Library of Congress Control Number: **2012937837**

Hardcover ISBN 978-0-8280-2589-8
Wire-O ISBN 978-0-8280-2684-0

Acknowledgments

My sincere thanks to:

Deanna Willett, an outstanding cook and teacher, who shared with me the basics of vegan cuisine and whose creative talent inspired me to develop recipes of my own.

The countless health guests and seminar participants who not only complimented my cooking, but who implemented lifestyle changes and regained their health, thereby encouraging me to keep cooking and sharing.

The Potomac Conference of Seventh-day Adventists and the Ardmore Institute of Health, parent corporation of the Lifestyle Center of America, who together enabled me to begin sharing this powerful message of healthful living through the **StepFast Lifestyle Series**.

Gladys Copeland, Barbara Hesslegrave and Jean Marie Smith for lending their editorial skills and providing valuable feedback.

My family and friends for tolerating many culinary experiments and giving me honest opinions and helpful suggestions.

The many friends who have shared recipe ideas with me over the years, including Zinia Agosto, Julianne Aranda, the Benton sisters, Melissa Bradshaw, Kae Borrero, Dan and Ellen Butler, Janet Evert, Raquel Garcia, Geraldine Hollis, Kathy Mountjoy, Erica Nedley, Pat Pagan, Robert Pannekoek, Dyane Pergerson, Joann Rachor, Paula Reiter, Ronda Smith, Peggy Spangler, Sebastian Teh, and others.

My daughter Charlotte (Charlie), for sharing her talent in food styling, her exceptional organizational skills, and her positive attitude, all of which made writing this book a fun project and helped tremendously in getting it to press.

Amazing Facts, whose effective and far-reaching ministry addresses the needs of the whole person, for making the publishing of this book possible.

René Paille, my wonderful husband, for his love and encouragement and for the beautiful images of the recipes.

Most importantly, my heavenly Father, for all that He has taught me about His marvelous plan for health, happiness, and the eternal abundant life, and for giving me so many wonderful opportunities to share these principles with others.

Introduction

"Moses was one hundred and twenty years old when he died.
His eyes were not dim nor his natural vigor abated."
—Deuteronomy 34:7 (NKJV)

Even Moses had to die, but what a way to go! After living six score years, the weathered but wiry patriarch climbed a mountain. There, in the clean desert air and under blue skies, he viewed the Promised Land with crystal clear eyes. Then he simply lay down . . . and died. During his pilgrimage in the wilderness, Moses followed all the Bible secrets for a longer, stronger life — fresh air, exercise, a good diet, and trust in God, just to name a few. Even though healthful living might not eliminate the prospect of death, it can certainly postpone it and greatly improve the quality of the life we do live! Moses was active and lucid even on his last day: He "went up from the plains of Moab to Mount Nebo, to the top of Pisgah, which is across from Jericho" (Deuteronomy 34:1 NKJV). It shouldn't take 10 years to die. One of the main reasons for America's health crisis is that through poor living habits, most people invite an unsavory assortment of disabling diseases. Plagued with a pandemic of diabetes, cancer, and heart disease, it seems that many people spend their last 10, 20, or even 30 years dying! Moreover, these self-destructive lifestyles have led to overcrowded hospitals, astronomical medical costs, and a virtually bankrupt government. People are so stressed, they can't sleep, as antacids fly off the shelf and the number of handicap parking places seems to climb. It doesn't need to be this way. It can change.

Indeed, people want good health, (comma only, omit elipsis . . .) but they are clearly confused about where to find it. According to the U.S. Food and Drug Administration, the public has 30,000 health supplements available to them on the market, representing a multibillion dollar industry. Indeed, more than 150 million Americans take some form of health supplement each year. While taking a vitamin pill or herbal supplement may be helpful at times, surely it's not a substitute for a healthy lifestyle. Often, people are looking for health in all the wrong places, while wasting a small fortune along the way.

Yet please consider that human physiology hasn't changed since the days of Moses, and those health secrets that worked for Moses also sustained an entire nation of people. In fact, after the Israelites traveled through the wilderness, following God's health plan along the way, the Bible records, "There was not one feeble person among their tribes" (Psalm 105:37).

Can you fathom that? A nation of more than 2 million citizens without one person in a clinic or nursing home. Imagine the boon to our nation's health and financial situation if we would all just follow the free health plan found in the Bible. And it can start with you!

These Bible secrets of health—each summarized in this book—are not composed of mysterious rituals or strange (omit herbal) concoctions. They are real, proven principles backed by modern science. We only call them "secrets" here because they have been neglected and buried by time and culture. Whatever your age, and regardless of your current health, adopting these free, simple principles can truly lead you to a longer and stronger . . . and happier . . . life.

Though each health principle holds vital importance, proper nutrition is presented first, as it plays a 'foundational role in the health we enjoy. The recipes in the Amazing Health Cookbook are designed for you to enjoy, while putting into practice the principles learned. Prepare them and share them with friends and neighbors and those you love, so they, too, can enjoy amazing health!

Table of Contents

BEVERAGES

BREAKFAST

BREADS & SUCH

SPREADS & DIPS

SALADS & SALAD DRESSINGS

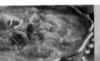

SOUPS & STEWS

ENTRÉES

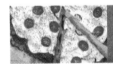

KIDS' STUFF

SIDES & SAUCES

CAKES & BAKES

SWEET TOPPINGS

PUDDINGS & PIES

FROZEN TREATS

Nutrition

What was the original diet for humanity?

According to the Bible, after Creation, Adam and Eve were instructed to eat fruits, grains, and nuts. God also instructed them to eat vegetables: "You shall eat the herb of the field" (Genesis 3:18, NKJV). These were the original God-given dietary plans for those living up to the time of the Flood.

Following the Flood, because of the global obliteration of vegetation, a total plant-based diet was impossible for Noah and his family. In order to provide a consistent food source, God allowed for the eating of meat. However, God also designated the healthiest variety of animal for consumption, referring to these as "clean." (See Leviticus 11; Deuteronomy 14:3-21.) Indeed, instead of going into the ark in twos, clean animals went in by sevens!

Even though it was necessary at the time, meat eating apparently contributed to a tremendous decline in longevity. Before the Flood human life spans remained steady at around 900 years (Genesis 5). After the Flood we find that Noah's son Shem lived to be 600. Just nine generations later Abraham lived to be just 175. Today the average life expectancy is just a fraction of that of our pre-Flood ancestors. But if a diet rich in fruits, vegetables, nuts, seeds, and whole grains positively affected our pre-Flood ancestor's longevity, could a return to the original diet extend our lives today?

WHAT DO YOU NEED TO KNOW ABOUT NUTRITION?
The five basic components of food are carbohydrates, proteins, fats, vitamins, and minerals.

Carbohydrates are sources of starches, sugars, and fiber. Starch and sugar are converted into glucose, which is the body's main fuel. Fiber, found primarily in plant foods, acts as a bulking agent that helps keep the intestines clean.

Proteins are broken down by the body and converted into amino acids, which are the building blocks for hormones, enzymes, and structural components of the body, such as muscle tissue.

Fats are the most concentrated form of energy, supplying more than twice as many calories per gram than protein or carbohydrates. It can also be stored efficiently for later use. The three natural types of fats are monounsaturated, polyunsaturated, and saturated. The unsaturated fats are by far the healthiest form, especially when they come from plant sources. Diets rich in refined saturated fats have been linked with numerous diseases.

Vitamins and minerals are essential components of our diet. Whole foods, which have been refined as little as possible, naturally contain the highest amount of these nutrients. Phytochemicals, found only in plants, are added bonuses thought to play a role in the prevention of many diseases.

Don't you need some cholesterol in your diet?

Cholesterol comes packaged in different ways. High density lipoprotein (HDL) is the healthy form of cholesterol and actually helps to remove bad cholesterol from the body, returning it to the liver for recycling. Here's a simple way to remember the good and bad of cholesterol: HDL is "healthy," LDL is "lousy," and VLDL is "very lousy."

Cholesterol is found only in meat and animal products, such as milk and eggs. However, newborn babies are the only humans who actually need a dietary source of cholesterol—which ideally comes from breast milk! Because of the liver's ability to produce cholesterol, we simply don't need a dietary source of cholesterol past breastfeeding age.

Diabetes: Is it true that diabetes is caused by eating sugar?

If eating simple carbohydrates (highly refined foods, such as sugar) contributes to excess body weight, then yes, the risk of type 2 diabetes is increased. However, research has shown that consuming complex plant-based carbohydrates (food as grown) actually reduces the risk of developing diabetes. One study of 36,000 women in Iowa found that those who ate the largest amounts of unrefined carbohydrates and fiber had the least incidence of diabetes. Furthermore, a study conducted at the National Public Health Institute in Finland found that people who ate the largest quality of whole grains had a 61 percent less risk of developing diabetes!

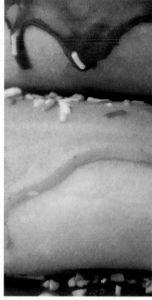

What about fat?

The two most significant risk factors in developing diabetes have to do with fat. Being overweight is one risk factor, but the most prominent factor is consuming large amounts of dietary fat. A study involving 1,300 Colorado residents determined that those with low-carbohydrate, high-fat diets were much more likely to develop diabetes. In another study of young men, researchers fed high-fat, low-carb diets to one group and a high-carb, low-fat diet to another. The group with the high-fat diet developed "chemical diabetes," but the low-fat group had no signs of diabetes by the conclusion of the study.

Eating highly refined foods has also been shown to increase the risk of developing diabetes. One study determined that consumption of partially hydrogenated oils is responsible for approximately 40 percent of all cases of type 2 diabetes in the United States!

Cancer: Does food impact your risk?

Fruits and vegetables are high in vitamins, fiber, and antioxidants—some of the best cancer-fighting ingredients that exist. In fact, one study found that men who eat three or more servings of cruciferous vegetables (broccoli, cauliflower, etc.) per week lowered their risk of prostate cancer by 41 percent. The World Cancer Research Fund found that people who consumed five or more servings of fruits and vegetables a day reduced cancer risk by approximately 50 percent. Vegetables, in particular, were found to help prevent cancers of the rectum and colon.

Conversely, diets rich in red meat and cholesterol have been linked to colon cancer. In fact, a study of 88,751 American nurses found that those consuming red meat daily were 2.5 times more likely to develop colon cancer than those who consumed less than 1 serving per month.

Finally, numerous studies have shown the relationship between a high-sugar diet and cancer. High sugar intake has been linked to an increased risk of cancers of the colon, rectum, breast, ovaries, uterus, prostate, kidney, as well as cancers of the central nervous system. One of the reasons suggested for sugar's effect on cancer is that sugar weakens the immune system. A study published by the Southern California Dental Association found that after consuming only 24 teaspoons of sugar, the ability of white blood cells to destroy bacteria was decreased by 92 percent!

> **AMAZING HEALTH FACTS**
>
> Even though God permitted the eating of meat, He warned people not to eat meat that still has its lifeblood in it (Genesis 9:4; Leviticus 3:17; 1 Samuel 14:32–34). Indeed, some tribes in Africa, such as the Maasai, consume blood as part of their diet. Autopsies performed on 50 Maasai men showed extensive heart disease. Though their extremely physical lifestyle offers some protection, they still have the worst life expectancy in the modern world (45 years for women and 42 years for men).

Mental Health: Food for thought?

Not only is a meat and dairy diet a risk factor for cardiovascular disease, but studies have actually shown that elevated levels of cholesterol can affect mental health. One study revealed that elevated levels of cholesterol are a significant factor in mild cognitive impairment.

Diet also plays a significant role in the development of Alzheimer's disease: Consuming large amounts of partially hydrogenated fats increases the risk of Alzheimer's by almost 2.5 times. Another study revealed that eating meat increased the diseases associated with metabolic syndrome, characterized by high insulin levels, which may also trigger Alzheimer's disease.

Can soft drinks contribute to a weight problem?

Yes, big-time! Soft drinks are the largest source of sugar in the American diet. In fact, daily soft drink consumption adds roughly 9 teaspoons of sugar to the diet of adolescent girls and about 14 teaspoons for adolescent boys. According to the USDA, sugar consumption has been steadily increasing since 1982, with highly refined foods as the largest contributor. The average 12-ounce can of soda has 10 teaspoons of sugar, but even white bread contains roughly 3 teaspoons per slice!

A plant-based diet might sound bland . . . but you can transition tastefully!

If you feel like the satisfaction of a meat diet could be worth the health risk, *stop!* True, a slice of tofu tastes different than sirloin steak, but eating a plant-based diet doesn't have to be, and ideally shouldn't be, a tasteless diet. Fortunately this book contains delicious, plant-based recipes that will help you make the transition. Living longer and stronger really is worth the investment!

The Bread of Life

Complex carbohydrates, omega-3 fatty acids, vitamins, minerals, phytonutrients, and even a plant-based diet might give us a better quality of life and increase our longevity. However, there is one thing that we all will eventually face: death. If there was a food that promised to reverse the ravages of death and give eternal youth, would you eat it? There is only one "food" that promises such results.

"Jesus said to them, 'I am the bread of life. He who comes to Me shall never hunger. . . . And the one who comes to Me I will by no means cast out' " (John 6:35-37, NKJV). What He said to His disciples 2,000 years ago, Jesus also says to you today.

Do you desire to come to Him? He has promised not to send you away hungry. Visit w**ww. AmazingHealthFacts.org** to discover more about nutrition and everlasting life.

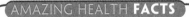

Exercise

How do I target heart health?

Heart fitness is best achieved through exercise that keeps your heart rate within age-specific parameters—your "target heart rate." Your specific target heart rate can be calculated using this formula:

220 - your age = target heart rate in beats per minute.

For example, the target heart rate for a 40-year-old is 180 beats per minute.

220 - 40 (years old) = 180 beats per minute.

To get your heart as healthy as possible, your pulse rate needs to stay between 50 to 75 percent of your target heart rate during sustained aerobic activity.

AMAZING HEALTH **FACTS**

Intermittent training (IT) is an exercise style characterized by intense activity followed by a short period of rest. Researchers have found that this type of exercise is able to increase aerobic capacity (the amount of oxygen your body can use) and reduce fatigue better than sustained exercise.

Confused about target heart rate? Let's talk . . .

If you don't feel comfortable calculating your target heart rate or taking your pulse, try the "conversational heart rate" approach. If you can exercise and carry on a basic conversation, you are probably exercising in your target zone. But if you can sing while you exercise, you probably are not exercising hard enough. If you are winded and have to take breaks to catch your breath between words, you probably are exercising too hard. This method works best for moderate intensity exercises, such as walking.

What if my main goal is to lose weight?

If you want to lose weight, remember this important equation: Calories going in must be less than calories lost. In other words, to lose weight, your energy expenditure must be more than the number of calories you eat.

Did you know that your body is constantly burning calories, even while sleeping? The rate at which your body uses calories simply to stay alive is known as "basal metabolic rate" (BMR). Studies have shown that building more muscle mass, through weight training, actually increases BMR—which means your body will naturally burn more calories in a day. Aerobic exercise, such as brisk walking, will burn additional calories per hour on top of your BMR. So a regular exercise routine that alternates between aerobic and anaerobic exercise is best for sustained weight loss.

Another important consideration for burning fat is exercise intensity: It should be moderate, not intense. During moderate exercise, fat is used as energy, but during intense exercise, carbohydrate (glucose) becomes the fuel of choice.

How can I get enough exercise with my busy schedule?

You might find it easier simply to start the day earlier with exercise. Experts believe the early morning is the

CHECK WITH YOUR DOCTOR BEFORE BEGINNING A NEW EXERCISE PROGRAM!

optimal time to exercise, because air quality is generally better then. Plus, follow-through with an exercise routine has been shown to be greater for those exercising in the morning.

Too much of a good thing . . .

Increasing your exercise intensity should be a gradual process. In fact, for those living a sedentary lifestyle, a sudden high intensity workout can be deadly. In one study, researchers estimated that almost half of all heart attacks are triggered by strenuous physical effort. The study found that those who were less active were at much greater risk for a heart attack following strenuous exercise than those on a regular exercise routine.

Obesity: Can exercise really help lose the extra weight?

One of the risk factors for developing obesity is a sedentary lifestyle. For weight loss to occur, remember that energy output must be greater than energy intake—and the best way to increase energy output is exercise.

Plus, regular moderate exercise is also important in sustaining weight loss. A study by the National Weight Control Registry found that 91 percent of those who had sustained weight loss followed a regular exercise routine, such as an hour of brisk walking each day.

Can exercise also reverse diabetes?

Lifestyle centers, such as the Weimar Center of Health and Education in California, have had tremendous success in reversing diabetes. These physician-monitored programs stress health education, exercise, a healthy diet, and other lifestyle factors helpful in reaching optimal health.

Studies have shown that exercise in particular has an immediate and prolonged effect on blood sugar among diabetics. One study reported that the benefits of increased glucose use lasted several hours after exercise. Another study revealed that the body's own insulin, which suffers from impaired function among type 2 diabetics, actually improved in function for up to 16 hours following moderate exercise.

IF YOU ARE TAKING DIABETES MEDICATION, CHECK FIRST WITH YOUR PHYSICIAN BEFORE BEGINNING ANY EXERCISE PROGRAM.

Exercise of a Different Variety

As you have seen, in order to promote health and prevent disease, we need to exercise routinely. But did you know that there is another form of exercise that yields eternal rewards?

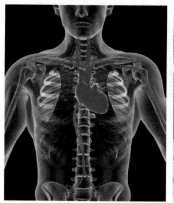

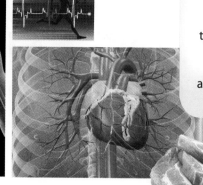

"For bodily exercise profits a little, but godliness is profitable for all things, having promise of the life that now is and of that which is to come" (1 Timothy 4:8, NKJV).

Just as we must exercise to promote bodily health, we must exercise godliness to receive the promise of spiritual and eternal health. To reach this goal, we are called upon to exercise faith.

One New Testament writer put it this way:

"Let us lay aside every weight, and the sin which so easily ensnares us, and let us run with endurance the race that is set before us, looking unto Jesus, the author and finisher of our faith, who for the joy that was set before Him endured the cross, despising the shame, and has sat down at the right hand of the throne of God" (Hebrews 12:1, 2, NKJV).

WOULD YOU LIKE TO KNOW HOW TO LAY DOWN THE BURDENS IN YOUR LIFE?

"But those who wait on the Lord shall renew their strength; They shall mount up with wings like eagles, they shall run and not be weary, they shall walk and not faint" (Isaiah 40:31, NKJV).

That's good advice, both physically and spiritually — so why not start an exercise program as soon as possible? Visit www.AmazingHealthFacts.org for more about physical and spiritual exercise.

Water

What happens to our bodies when we don't have enough water?

Our bodies have an intricate defense mechanism to protect vital organs from periods of inadequate water. The body takes water from less-vital areas (skin, joints, bones, etc.) and gives it to the brain, heart, and other organs.

Unfortunately, many people live their entire lives in a partially dehydrated condition—resulting in premature aging, stress on kidneys, arthritis, and a host of other health problems.

How much water do we really need?

It is important to drink water regularly and consistently, even long before you feel thirsty.

The following recommendations, from the World Health Organization (WHO), are for daily water intake under normal environmental conditions:

Females: Approximately 9 eight-ounce glasses
Males: Approximately 12 eight-ounce glasses

On average, 4 percent of the body's water is lost per day. Water is lost through urine, bowel movements, sweating, and breathing. Of course copious sweating and breathing from exercise will necessitate additional water intake slightly above the normal recommendations.

Why can't we drink water simply when we're thirsty?

Do you wait to drink water until you feel thirsty? According to experts, you are probably suffering from dehydration (too little water) long before your brain tells you to drink something.

Is it really that easy to become dehydrated?

It is very easy to become dehydrated. Going one day without adequate water can cause moderate dehydration. Going two days without water could result in a life-threatening case of dehydration.

WHAT ARE SOME OF THE EARLY SYMPTOMS OF DEHYDRATION?

Mild dehydration is a 1 to 3 percent reduction in body weight as a result of fluid loss and can cause:

headache,

fatigue,

confusion,

flushed skin,

loss of appetite,

heat intolerance,

light-headedness,

dry mouth and eyes,

lack of skin elasticity,

stomach pains, which could be confused with hunger,

and a slower metabolism, which can result in weight gain.

Cardiovascular disease: Can water help your heart?

A recent study that included more than 20,000 participants discovered that men who drank more than five 8-ounce glasses of water a day cut their risk of heart disease by 46 percent. The number was even greater for women: 59 percent!

Cancer: can water make a difference in cancer prevention?

Adequate water intake has an incredible preventative effect on colon cancer. One study reported that adequate water intake reduced the incidence of colon cancer in men by 92 percent. Another study found that postmenopausal women who drank more than five glasses of water a day lowered their risk of breast cancer by 79 percent. Research has also shown that individuals can lower their risk of bladder cancer by 51 percent simply by drinking enough water.

Urinary tract health: is more water (and bathroom breaks!) really necessary?

Your kidneys are sophisticated filters that process about 200 quarts of blood each day to sift out about two quarts of waste products. The only substance that properly cleans the kidneys is water. According to the National Kidney Research Fund, increasing your water intake to approximately eight 8-ounce glasses a day is the best way to ensure proper kidney function, avoid kidney stones, flush impurities from the blood, and protect against urinary tract infections.

Water Inside and Out

In this section you've seen the multiple health benefits of water on the inside, but don't neglect the benefits of water on the outside. In fact, external cleanliness is the single greatest health advancement made in all of modern history. In the 1860s Dr. Joseph Lister read in the Bible that Moses commanded his people to wash with water after touching anything unclean (Leviticus 22:6). When Lister suggested that surgeons wash their hands and their instruments before operating, at first he was mocked as eccentric. But when death from infection was cut 75 percent in his hospital, Lister's obsession with washing soon became the standard. Daily washing of the body with water and frequent washing of the hands can help prevent a virtual encyclopedia of ills.

Living Water

As important as water is to our health, something else is even more important: In the Bible, Jesus is called the Living Water who provides eternal life. In the same way that many people go through life chronically dehydrated, many more go through life spiritually dehydrated. Like

AMAZING HEALTH **FACTS**

Drinking other beverages (fruit juice, coffee, tea, etc.) does not provide the same health benefits as plain water. In fact, research has shown that women who consume large quantities of non-water beverages increased their risk of a fatal heart attack by two-and-a-half times. The same study showed that men increased their risk by 50 percent!

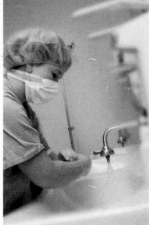

"For He draws up drops of water, which distill as rain from the mist, which the clouds drop down and pour abundantly on man" (Job 36:27, 28, NKJV).

the altered thirst sensation that many mistake as hunger, many mistakenly discern spiritual thirst for hunger after the things of this world.

Speaking of water, Jesus said, "Whoever drinks of this water will thirst again, but whoever drinks of the water that I shall give him will never thirst. But the water that I shall give him will become in him a fountain of water springing up into everlasting life" (John 4:13, 14, NKJV). This offer was not only for the people of His day, but also for you: "Let him who thirsts come. Whoever desires, let him take the water of life freely" (Revelation 22:17, NKJV).

To learn more about this water that will never leave you thirsty again, visit **www.AmazingHealthFacts.org**

Sunlight

What's so good about light?

Light is essential to all life—so essential that God provided in the sun a constant source to supply the energy necessary to sustain all life on earth. The energy used by plants growing in your garden, a cheetah running at top speed, and even the gasoline that powers your car can all be traced back to the energy supplied by sunlight. In fact, solar power is the originator of nearly all naturally occurring energy on the earth.

Yet even though God said that light was good in the beginning, many people are actually afraid of sun exposure today. Perhaps we have been so misinformed that we are overreacting to the dangers of sunlight while missing the many positive health benefits. "Truly the light is sweet, and a pleasant thing it is for the eyes to behold the sun" (Ecclesiastes 11:7).

Can sunlight actually improve health?

Like plants, human beings also need sunlight for optimal health. Although many believe that any exposure to sunlight is harmful, it is actually an overexposure to direct sunlight that should be avoided.

SUN
protection

In fact, in moderation, sunlight can . . .

- *increase immunity,*
- *prevent diseases,*
- *improve sleep,*
- *increase mental performance,*
- *heighten metabolism,*
- *relieve arthritic pains,*
- *and boost energy levels.*

Many of sunlight's benefits are connected to vitamin D. Our bodies must have the UVB radiation found in sunlight to make this essential, health-promoting vitamin.

When exposed to sunlight, our skin begins to protect itself from overexposure by producing melanin, a chemical that darkens skin, and vitamin D precursors. Increased melanin and vitamin D allows increased exposure to the sun without burning.

How much sun exposure do I need?

Approximately 30 minutes a day, three times a week, in direct sunlight is adequate for most Caucasians. The darker your skin, the more sun exposure you need to obtain an adequate amount of vitamin D. However, if you have very fair skin, burn easily, or live in areas where the sun is particularly intense, you will want to make sun exposure a gradual process. If reddening of the skin occurs, you may have spent too much time in the sun!

Start with as little as five minutes per day (for the fair-skinned) and gradually increase exposure to 30 minutes or more per day. If you stay out in the sun for longer periods of time, be sure to wear a wide-brimmed hat and clothes that will protect the areas of your body that are most likely to get burned (face, ears, neck, shoulders, and back). Be aware, however, that barriers that reduce ultraviolet (UV) radiation (sunscreen, windows, etc.) also will reduce vitamin D production in your body!

Too much of a good thing . . .

Remember, sunlight is best in moderation. Protein and genetic tissue are damaged each time your skin burns, putting you at greater risk for skin cancer.

However, don't let this scare you away from obtaining proper sun exposure! The body will make adequate vitamin D with only one quarter of the sunlight required to cause a sunburn.

And although skin cancer claims the lives of approximately 2,000 Americans per year, researchers believe that regular, moderate exposure to the sun can actually prevent 138,000 deaths from other types of cancer each year.

Cancer: Can sunlight actually prevent cancer?

Exposure to sunlight has also been found to prevent certain cancers. One study concluded that moderate sunlight exposure decreased colon cancer risk by up to 80 percent. Indeed, vitamin D is believed to actually stop a variety of cancer cells from growing—including leukemia, lymphoma, and melanoma (skin cancer).

Diabetes: How does sunlight affect diabetes?

Vitamin D also has an incredible preventative effect against juvenile diabetes. One study found that children in Finland given a vitamin D supplement had an 88 percent less chance to develop type 1 diabetes. (This study was done in Finland because of the limited sunlight the nation's children receive nine months out of the year. Vitamin D supplements are not necessary for a child who receives adequate sun exposure.)

Another study of American adults showed a benefit of adequate sunlight exposure on numerous type 2 diabetes risk factors. Most notably, adequate intake of vitamin D reduced the risk of obesity. The study also showed that

kidney function was significantly increased by good levels of vitamin D.

Skin Health:
Isn't sunlight bad for our skin?

Sunlight is antibacterial, antiviral, and antifungal. Thus, in moderation, it's absolutely beneficial for certain skin conditions, such as acne, athlete's foot, and viral skin infections.

But remember three important considerations for sunlight and skin health: moderation, moderation, moderation. Frequent and excessive tanning can cause skin to dry, wrinkle, and prematurely age your skin. If you want to be

good to your skin, avoid overexposure and underexposure!

Sleep Disorders:
How can sunshine help you sleep better?

Believe it or not, sunlight can help you sleep better at night. When sunlight enters the retina of your eye, it triggers the pineal gland to convert sleep-enhancing (melatonin) hormones to those that increase alertness (serotonin). Similarly, moderate exposure to sunlight has been found to regulate these hormones effectively and will help you get a better night's rest!

Mental Health and Fatigue:
Can sunlight help you think better?

When the body's hormones are functioning optimally, sunlight causes the production of melatonin to decrease and serotonin to increase. Not only is serotonin the chemical the brain uses to produce alertness—it also helps create a feeling of happiness. That's why experts recommend waking up early: so you can take full advantage of a day's worth of natural light!

The Best Light in the World!

"God is light, and in him is no darkness at all" (1 John 1:5).

We have seen that sunlight is essential to good physical and mental health. However, could there be another type of light that is essential for our spiritual well-being?

According to the Bible, Jesus created the physical world: "He was in the beginning with God. All things were made through Him, and without Him nothing was made that was made" (John 1:2, 3, NKJV). And in the Creation account itself, it was the Word of God that first gave light to the world—because the sun, moon, and stars were created on the fourth day.

Interestingly, then, Christ is often referred to as the "Word" (John 1:14). It must be no coincidence that Jesus also says, "As long as I am in the world, I am the light of the world" (John 9:5, NKJV).

Scientists believe that someday the sun will burn out. However, Jesus desires to give us light now beyond that which is seen: "Then Jesus spoke to them again, saying, 'I am the light of the world. He who follows Me shall not walk in darkness, but have the light of life' " (John 8:12, NKJV).

Just as sunlight has powerful healing potential for our bodies, Jesus, the light of the world, is the best "Sunshine Vitamin" for our souls. "To you who fear My name the Sun of Righteousness shall arise with healing in His wings" (Malachi 4:2, NKJV).

Visit **www.AmazingHealthFacts.org** to learn more about the Light of the world, who provides eternal health!

Temperance

The Frontal Lobe

In September 1848 a 25-year-old railroad foreman, Phineas P. Gage, was using an iron rod to pack explosive powder into a hole when a powerful blast propelled the 13-pound tamping iron like a bullet through his head. Amazingly, this traumatic accident did not kill Phineas. In fact, he regained his physical strength and lived for another 13 years. He also seemed mentally sound: he could speak and do physical tasks just as well as before, and his memory seemed unimpaired.

Yet friends and family knew he was no longer the same man. Before the accident he was a well-loved, responsible worker and husband. He was known by all as a pious and dependable man. But after the accident, Phineas experienced a major moral decline. He became very short-tempered, rude, and foul-mouthed. He started to smoke and drink and lost all respect for spiritual things. It seemed as though his ethical filters had been turned off.

Phineas' accident ended up costing him his moral standards and his commitment to loved ones. Researchers have concluded that he had lost a very important part of his brain called the "frontal lobe," a large section of the brain that is responsible for moral reasoning, judgment, social behavior, and spirituality. Did you know that the Bible talks about a mark in the forehead that can mean the difference between life and death?

WHAT HAPPENS WHEN THE FRONTAL LOBE MALFUNCTIONS?

Experts have linked frontal lobe damage with schizophrenia, bipolar disorder, obsessive-compulsive disorder, depression, and numerous other mental illnesses. Some of the effects of frontal lobe damage can include:

- impairment of moral principle,
- social impairment,
- lack of foresight,
- loss of abstract reasoning,
- diminished ability for math,
- lack of restraint (boasting, hostility, aggressiveness),
- memory impairment (especially of recent events),
- distractibility and restlessness,
- emotional instability,
- apathy (lack of initiative), and
- indifference to one's condition (happy-go-lucky).

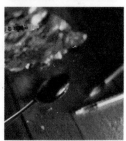

Where are decisions really made?

The frontal lobe of the brain is the key to our rational, moral, and ethical decision-making. It is the part of the brain that defines our character, personality, and will. Essentially, the frontal lobe is the section of our minds that contains our spiritual nature. Because of this, Satan is constantly trying to destroy or cloud this part of the brain.

Does alcohol impair decision-making?

Alcohol use is responsible for millions of cases of disabling mental illness each year. Often overlooked, one factor affects 100 percent of alcohol users: frontal lobe impairment.

The neurotransmitter responsible for halting an action or nerve impulse in the brain is known as "gamma-aminobutyric acid" (GABA). Alcohol blocks the action of GABA at the nerve junction, enabling you to do things your conscience wouldn't normally allow. This results in an increase of risky behaviors, aggression, and impulsivity. Eventually, these actions might even become habitual. The more times a neuron carries out an impulse, the more likely it is to allow the same action.

The results can be lethal: One study revealed that alcohol intoxication increases the risk of suicide by 90 times! Worse yet, alcohol can alter neuron DNA, thereby passing brain damage down from generation to generation.

Many "social drinkers" mistakenly believe that alcohol makes them more confident. Yet confidence has to do with the execution of a task without anxiety. Those who rely on alcohol for certain tasks have never actually built up the confidence through logical decision-making. And during acute intoxication, you are more of a passenger than a driver. Bottom line: If you value your ability to make rational decisions, steer completely clear of alcohol!

Isn't moderate alcohol use good for health?

Alcohol is responsible for up to 30 percent of the worldwide incidence of esophageal cancer, liver cancer, liver cirrhosis, homicide, epileptic conditions, and

automobile accidents. In fact, alcohol consumption is a likely cause of more than 60 different types of diseases and disabilities. It is estimated that alcohol use results in 1.8 million deaths annually worldwide. And heavy drinkers are not the only ones affected—even social drinkers die younger than nondrinkers.

Alcohol is not a harmless social beverage, but rather a mind-altering, addictive drug. It is mistaken to suggest that drinking alcohol is nothing more than a benign personal choice. Alcohol consumption is involved in half of all murders, half of all violent crime, one third of all child abuse, one third of all suicides, more than half of all domestic violence, half of all traffic deaths, and a large portion of unwanted pregnancies, sexual assaults, and divorces! It is the world's most destructive drug and costs U.S. taxpayers nearly $200 billion a year!

How do people get addicted?

Did you know that your brain is naturally wired for pleasure? This isn't a bad thing, because the pleasure circuit of the brain can help reinforce healthy behavior, such as exercising, reading, productive hobbies, etc.

However, certain substances can take over this natural process and lead to addiction. Addiction is characterized by two distinct processes: tolerance and dependence.

- **TOLERANCE** means that the brain becomes accustomed to the pleasurable stimulation and demands increasing levels to achieve the same response.
- **DEPENDENCE** describes the adverse emotional and physical reactions that occur after the pleasing stimulation is removed.

Research has shown that illicit drugs, such as cocaine, and even many "legal" drugs, can cause permanent structural changes in both brain cells and genetic material. Using an addictive drug can actually alter the brain cells to become more sensitive to other addictive substances. Thus, when new drugs are used, they create an even more intense pleasure response, leading to stronger future addictions.

Chemicals released in this runaway pleasure response, such as the protein dynorphin, actually depress the entire pleasure response system. Thus, ordinary pleasurable experiences lose their appeal. Addictive drugs become the pleasure of choice: an all-consuming desire. Because of genetic damage, children can inherit heightened sensitivity to addictive drugs. If you have great-grandparents, grandparents, or parents who abused alcohol, tobacco, or any other kind of addictive drug, you are at much greater risk for forming strong addictions.

Can caffeine affect your judgment?

Since caffeine binds itself to receptors that inhibit certain impulses, the activity of stimulating neurotransmitters is increased. This neurotransmitter imbalance can lead to mental illnesses caused by an increased amount of the neurotransmitter dopamine.

Is caffeine robbing your sleep?

Caffeine comes from a family of chemicals called methylxanthines.
In high doses,

AMAZING HEALTH **FACTS**

One study found that young people who consumed more than five caffeinated beverages a day had almost twice the odds of developing a hemorrhagic stroke. The same study found that adults who took higher amounts of caffeine (in the form of caffeine-containing drugs) had almost four times the odds for a hemorrhagic stroke! (Hemorrhagic stroke occurs in almost 60,000 Americans every year and has a 50 percent mortality rate.)

caffeine is lethal to humans. In low doses, it can reduce fatigue, improve circulation, and many other stimulating effects. However, this extra stimulation comes at a high cost.

The word "homeostasis" describes the body's attempt to maintain balance and health. Naturally, periods of stimulation should be accompanied with periods of adequate rest. In fact, the body has several defense mechanisms to help maintain an optimal balance between stimulation and rest.

However, caffeine removes these defense mechanisms and allows the body to continue in a state of increased stimulation—even while sleeping! Studies have shown that as little as 200 mg of caffeine in the morning can impact sleep the following evening. Caffeine affects especially the deeper stages of sleep, when the brain is normally in a state of decreased activity.

Was tobacco ever healthy?

Although much is known today about the deadly and addictive effects of tobacco, years ago it was thought to be a healthy habit. Doctors even prescribed tobacco for its apparent benefits on mood and physical vigor.

Over time, of course, increasing evidence revealed the health risks of tobacco use. However, tobacco companies still denied that their products were related to death, disease, or addiction. In fact, it took decades for them to admit that cigarettes were harmful and addictive. Moreover, we now know that these companies had ample evidence that their products were dangerous. As a result, tobacco companies were sued and legislation was passed demanding that these companies label their products as addictive and harmful.

Yet surprisingly, many still buy their deadly products!

Do tobacco companies care about health?

Despite being forced to pour millions of dollars into stop-smoking campaigns, tobacco companies continue to spend billions of dollars each year on advertising and marketing. The bottom line is that if tobacco companies really cared about your health, they would close up shop instead of recruiting new victims.

Today we have to make the right choice—we can choose to be a victim or to abstain.

You can choose a better tree!

"The tree of life was also in the midst of the garden" (Genesis 2:9, NKJV).

In addition to the forbidden tree in the Garden of Eden, there was another magnificent tree—the tree of life, which had the power to provide eternal vitality and health to humanity.

Just as the two trees provided a choice for Adam and Eve in the garden, a similar choice is offered to everyone today. We can choose true wisdom and life; or we can choose deception, addiction, and death.

When God offered His Son as a sacrifice on the cross, He provided the only antidote for most deadly addiction of all time: the addiction of sin. The cross of Christ became a new tree of life and Jesus' perfect life the fruit. Jesus said, "Whoever eats My flesh and drinks My blood has eternal life" (John 6:54, NKJV). This means accepting His sacrifice for your sins, reading His Word, and believing His message of forgiveness and power.

Satan has been working as hard as he can to blind people from this "tree of life." The devil wants to take away your free choice. In fact, he hates your frontal lobe because it gives you the rational power to see past his deceptions!

Unfortunately, many have allowed their brains to become so clouded by bad habits that they are unable to clearly see the truth. But God promises you something real, something you can trust. In the end the decision is still clear, but this time it is yours. Make it with a clear mind! Reach out for the fruit of life and accept God's promises today! To learn more, visit **www. AmazingHealthFacts.org**

Air

Breathed Into Being

Looking closely at the biblical Creation account, you'll notice something very unique in how God created humanity. He formed Adam with His own hands and breathed His "breath of life" into his lungs. If the "breath of life" began our existence, it stands to reason the absence of that breath can terminate it.

As you will see, the air you choose to breathe and how well you breathe has a huge impact on how long you actually remain a living being: It can either be a "savor of life unto life" or "death unto death" (2 Corinthians 2:16). Take a deep breath and keep reading!

Why is air such a heavy subject?

Oxygen is our body's most important physical need. Although air is composed of only about 20 percent oxygen, each inhalation brings this life-sustaining gas into the lungs. Oxygen then diffuses into the bloodstream, where it is transported all over the body via your red blood cells. It is mostly used to facilitate reactions involving the body's main energy source: glucose. Without oxygen, this energy source would be useless.

Is there anything you can do to breathe better?

Fortunately, breathing is innate (we don't have to think about it), but many people have bad breathing habits and don't use their lungs effectively. Ideally, breathing should expand the lungs through lowering the diaphragm (a muscle separating the lungs from the abdominal organs). This can be accomplished by relaxing the abdominal muscles during inhalation. The idea is to expand your upper lungs as well as your lower lungs, resulting in increased lung capacity, "deeper breathing," and a more efficient oxygen/carbon dioxide exchange. In fact, the practice of deep breathing is one of the simplest ways of preventing certain types of pneumonia.

Too much of a good thing…

Rapid breathing during exercise is healthy and necessary because the body needs extra amounts of oxygen. However, hyperventilation (abnormally rapid breathing) caused by anxiety and nervousness can lead to an excess of oxygen in the blood and a corresponding decrease in carbon dioxide levels. When this happens, the body's pH balance is disturbed (known as "respiratory alkalosis"). Symptoms include dizziness and rapid heartbeat. A common treatment for hyperventilation is breathing into a paper bag, which restores normal carbon dioxide levels.

Cancer: Smoking causes cancer, but can polluted air do the same?

Worldwide, indoor air pollution is thought to cause more than 1.5 percent of the approximately 1 million lung cancer deaths per year.

It is also estimated that radon gas affects one out of every 15 homes in America. Why is this important? The American Lung Association rates radon as the second-leading cause of lung cancer in the United States—up to 20,000 lung cancer deaths per year, second only to smoking.

Radon test kits are widely available and inexpensive, but the single most effective way of increasing the quality of indoor air is proper ventilation. Other indoor contaminates such as formaldehyde (found in pressed-wood products, paneling, etc.) are estimated to contribute about 6,500 additional lung cancer deaths each year.

Mental Health: How does air affect your brain?

Keeping brain cells healthy is vital to combating mental health issues such as depression and anxiety, while improving overall mental performance. For this, the brain needs an almost constant supply of oxygen. If you are not adequately oxygenated, the brain will be the first to suffer. (Fainting is actually a defense mechanism to protect the brain from low oxygen levels.)

Lung disease/illnesses: WHO cares about bad air?

The World Health Organization (WHO) estimates that, globally, almost 700,000 of the 2.7 million deaths

from lung disease per year are caused by indoor air pollution. The WHO also estimates that exposure to indoor air pollution almost doubles the risk of pneumonia. In fact, indoor air pollution is estimated to cause more than 900,000 of the 2 million yearly pneumonia-related deaths worldwide.

Tried to quit but can't break the habit?

Did you know that smoking also affects mental health? Nicotine has been found to excessively increase serotonin levels, which causes anxiety. Perhaps this is one of the reasons researchers have linked the daily quantity of cigarettes smoked and an increase in anxiety disorders. When a person stops smoking, serotonin levels drop—a process that might lead to depression.

Unfortunately, nicotine withdrawal can also cause anxiety. Quitting smoking can temporarily make you totally miserable. This is part of the reason many can't seem to quit. Don't despair! There are many things you can do to bring your emotions back into balance.

What are some tips to prevent depression after you stop smoking?

Dr. Tim Arnott, from Lifestyle Centers of America, suggests the following to help improve mood and combat depression:

1. Eat a plant-based diet, which helps to raise serotonin levels.
2. Maximize serotonin levels by eating soybeans, pumpkin seeds, sesame seeds, almonds, and beans.
3. Get 30 minutes of exposure to bright sunlight in the morning or take two 15-minute walks outdoors between 9:00 a.m. and 3:00 p.m. daily.
4. Walk briskly for one hour six days a week.
5. Eat two or three tablespoons of freshly ground flaxseed daily.
6. Eat between a fourth and a half cup of English walnuts at breakfast and lunch.
7. Take a B-complex vitamin with your noon or evening meal.
8. Dismiss negative thoughts and speak nothing negative of others.

WHAT'S IN CIGARETTE SMOKE, ANYWAY?

Smoking not only causes cancer but numerous other diseases because of harmful chemicals found in cigarette smoke. Indeed, cigarette smoke contains more than 4,000 different chemicals, and many of these are known to cause cancer:

- formaldehyde, which is commonly used to preserve dead bodies,

- arsenic, which is used to kill rats,

- ammonia, which is used to clean toilets,

- acetone, which is used to remove nail polish,

- carbon monoxide, which also comes out of your car's exhaust pipe,

- and hydrogen cyanide, a poison used to execute people in gas chambers.

If you want to quit smoking, will it be easier if you taper off?

If you truly desire to quit smoking, the easiest way is to actually quit. Studies have shown that those who attempt to "taper off" cigarettes have more prolonged nicotine withdrawal symptoms than those who quit "cold turkey."

Make the decision today to stop smoking: Studies have shown that almost as soon as you quit, the body starts to heal. And after just a few years, the risk of related diseases, such as lung cancer, actually approach the disease rates of nonsmokers!

The Breath of Life

The emotional pain and turmoil caused by quitting smoking has been compared to the loss of a friend. If you find yourself in this condition, you don't have to despair. You can start building another, healthier friendship today. There is actually Someone else who has been waiting to fill that very void in your life and in your lungs.

"Thus says God the Lord, who created the heavens and stretched them out, who spread forth the earth and that which comes from it, who gives breath to the people on it, and spirit to those who walk on it" (Isaiah 42:5, NKJV).

For humanity, the spark of life was God's exhale—His Word breathed into a man. "When he had said this, he [Jesus] breathed on them, and saith unto them, Receive ye the Holy Ghost" (John 20:22).

Whether we realize it or not, we are all longing for something more than just optimal respiration. We were formed by a unique act for a very unique relationship. "He gives to all life, breath, and all things" (Acts 17:25, NKJV).

Why not take time today to see how this incredible relationship can bring a breath of fresh air into your life? Visit **www.AmazingHealthFacts.org!**

Rest

What's the trouble with troubled sleep?

An estimated 60 million Americans have trouble sleeping. Today, because of artificial lights, TV, the Internet, and the caffeine craze, people are sleeping about one hour less than their great-grandparents did. This figure might be startling in itself—but considering that proper sleep is one of the most important elements in the process of healing, America is also in for a disease-ridden wake-up call.

What role does melatonin play in sleep?

Melatonin is a hormone produced by the pineal gland in response to darkness. One of the most notable functions of this hormone is its antioxidant capabilities, providing protection from dangerous free radicals inside the cell nuclei. This helps to prevent damage to the cell's most vital component: DNA. Damage to DNA has been linked to a host of diseases, such as cancer.

SEVEN SIMPLE STEPS TO A RESTFUL NIGHT'S SLEEP

1. **Wake up with the sun:** Sunlight helps to increase levels of alertness, enhancing hormones such as serotonin. Exposure to sunlight also slows down melatonin. (Granted, this is a little harder for those who live in the extreme north, where there are only a few hours of daylight in the winter.)

2. **Eat a balanced diet rich in plant-based complex carbohydrates and tryptophan:** Foods rich in tryptophan are good not only for sleep but also for optimal daytime performance. Tryptophan, an amino acid, is necessary for the construction of numerous hormones, including serotonin and melatonin. Carbohydrates help tryptophan enter the brain. Tryptophan-rich foods include: tofu, pumpkin seeds, gluten flour, sesame seeds, almonds, black walnuts, and black-eyed peas.

3. **Find time for moderate physical exercise:** Exercise helps increase levels of certain hormones that have been found to enhance sleep.

4. **Avoid sleep-depriving substances (alcohol, caffeine, nicotine, etc.):** Alcohol robs the body of both REM and deep sleep, while caffeine interferes with sleep because of its stimulating properties. Tobacco users miss out on deeper sleep because of nicotine withdrawal during the night. Antidepressants can also decrease levels of REM sleep.

5. **Have an established, early bedtime:** Experts recommend going to sleep at least two and a half hours before midnight. A regular pattern of sleep is also important, even if you sleep during the day. Studies have found that night shift workers function better with an established sleep/wake cycle as opposed to a random schedule.

6. **Sleep in the dark:** To optimize melatonin, it is important to sleep in total darkness: Exposure to bright light, even for a few moments, can lower melatonin levels.

7. **Leave your worries behind:** Studies show that increased levels of emotional stress can cause poor-quality sleep. Those who pray and commit their troubles to God at night have more serenity and sleep better. "I will both lay me down in peace, and sleep: for thou, Lord, only makest me dwell in safety" (Psalm 4:8).

Too much of a good thing . . .

Although individual sleep requirements vary somewhat, excessive sleep can be detrimental to your health. Studies have routinely shown that among adults, sleeping more than nine hours per day increases the risk of many common diseases, as compared to a more healthful seven to eight hours per day.

YES. SLEEP IS AN ACTIVITY.

Sleep is much more than just a passive experience for your body. Although we might be resting, our body is engaged in another type of activity, a process that will bring restoration and healing to frazzled organs, nerves, and body tissues.

Sleep is characterized by a cycle of five increasingly deeper stages of sleep followed by periods of increased brain activity:

Stage 1: If you have ever driven a car while drowsy, you are well acquainted with this stage of very light sleep. The startle that often awakes drowsy drivers is an indication of having briefly entered stage 1 sleep.

Stage 2: In this stage eye movements cease and, for the most part, brain activity decreases (but does not stop).

Stage 3: This is the beginning of deep sleep. Slower brain waves, called delta waves, appear. Delta waves are similar to the brain activity during a deep coma and mark the resting state of the brain.

Stage 4: This stage is characterized by a further increase in delta wave activity. This is the deepest stage of sleep. Those awakening during this stage are very disoriented and groggy because the brain is not in an alert mode.

Stage 5: This sleep is characterized by rapid eye movement (REM), dreaming, arm and leg paralysis (so we don't act out our dreams), and increased heart rate and blood pressure. The brainwave pattern during REM sleep is very close to that of being awake.

The actual function of REM sleep is unknown. However, it is theorized that REM is a period of information processing, storing, and the improvement of brain efficiency. After going through several sleep cycles, we spend most of the remaining sleep time in REM, stage 2, and stage 1 sleep.

Cardiovascular Disease: Does proper rest contribute to your heart health?

In a study of American nurses, sleep duration was shown to have a significant impact on heart disease. Compared to those sleeping about eight hours a night, those sleeping less than five hours per night had a 39 percent greater risk of developing heart disease. Those sleeping six hours had an 18 percent increase. Women who slept more than nine hours increased their risk by 37 percent and increased their risk of heart attack by 45 percent.

Another study found that participants who slept less than 6.5 hours a night had 50 percent higher levels of insulin compared to those who slept between 7.5 and 8.5 hours per night. High insulin levels can result in weight gain, high blood pressure, and increased cholesterol—all three being contributing factors to cardiovascular disease!

Obesity: Can too little sleep put on the pounds?

Inadequate sleep has a profound effect on the risk for obesity. In a study of American women, compared to those who slept seven hours a night, women who slept less than five hours had a much greater risk of weight gain and obesity—up to 58 percent! The study concluded that those sleeping seven to eight hours per night had the lowest risk for major weight gain.

Indeed, researchers have found a relationship between the body's appetite control hormones and sleep duration. In one study, those sleeping less than five hours a night, as opposed to eight hours, had lower levels of leptin, an appetite-suppressing hormone. To make matters worse, they were also found to have increased levels of a hormone that stimulates the appetite—a total of a 30 percent increase in hunger-promoting hormone levels!

Mental Health: Does sleep affect my brain?

Increased anxiety, confusion, and even mental illness have been attributed to inadequate sleep. One study that looked at the sleeping patterns of nearly 8,000 people during the course of a year found that inadequate sleep significantly increased the risk of depression. The study also found that oversleeping significantly increased the odds of mental illness.

Special Report: The Rest of the Week

"On the seventh day God ended his work which he had made; and he rested on the seventh day from all his work which he had made. And God blessed the seventh day, and sanctified it: because that in it he had rested from all his work which God created and made" (Genesis 2:2, 3).

Amazing! All creation witnessed God take time off. But unlike us, God didn't rest because He was physically tired. Rather, according to the Bible, God reserved and sanctified the 24 hours at the end of the week for spiritual and physical refreshment. The first seventh day must have been very special to God and humanity. It was a way to spend time together, away from the cares of the week. In fact, when God spoke to Moses thousands of years after the first day of weekly rest, He reminded him of how the seventh day of the week was still to be recognized as a very important day:

"Remember the Sabbath day, to keep it holy. Six days you shall labor and do all your work, but the seventh day is the Sabbath of the Lord your God. In it you shall do no work: you, nor your son, nor your daughter, nor your male servant, nor your female servant, nor your cattle, nor your stranger who is within your gates. For in six days the Lord made the heavens and the earth, the sea, and all that is in them, and rested the seventh day. Therefore the Lord blessed the Sabbath day and hallowed it" (Exodus 20:8-11, NKJV).

Of course, the Sabbath involves spiritual rest, but could there actually be physical benefits from a weekly day of rest that we take for granted?

What is the best reason for a weekly day of rest?

After a long workweek, we can all use a little physical recreation, as in "re-creation." However, far exceeding all other reasons for a weekly rest day is the fact that God told us to remember to keep the seventh day holy!

The Bible is full of examples of those who remembered God's fourth commandment, reaping the benefits of both physical and mental rest: Moses, King David, the apostles, and Jesus Christ!

Before sin we see that there was no need for physical recovery from a draining week of labor. Yet God sanctioned the seventh day anyway as a time of special communion with the people of His creation. Thus, the weekly rest, the "Sabbath," is most important as a blessed day of optimal spiritual recovery.

Do you have heavy burdens that you carry throughout the week? Are you looking for a rest from guilt, fear, or sorrow? Or are you simply looking for something better in life? There is a way of life that offers hope, happiness, and healing: Jesus said, "Come unto me, all ye that labor and are heavy laden, and I will give you rest" (Matthew 11:28). Would you like to know how you can have better spiritual and physical rest? Visit **www.SabbathTruth.com** to discover more about the seventh-day rest!

Trust

"God hath dealt to every man the measure of faith" (Romans 12:3).

A placebo is something that looks like a legitimate drug but is really nothing more than colored water or a starch pill containing no medicinal value at all. These placebos are often given to a patient to reinforce an expectation that their condition will improve. Placebos are also used when testing the effectiveness of new drugs. Research has clearly shown that when patients take a substance that they sincerely believe will heal them, their symptoms often improve or completely disappear.

In fact, in one study doctors successfully eliminated warts by painting them with a brightly colored but inert dye, promising patients the warts would be gone when the color wore off. And in a study of asthmatics, researchers found they could produce dilation of the airways by simply telling people they were inhaling a powerful bronchodilator, even when they weren't. There are thousands of other well-documented examples of how a person's beliefs brought about real physical improvement.

AMAZING HEALTH **FACTS**

Want to live seven years longer? Start praying. As the May 2001 *Reader's Digest* reports, a nationwide study of 21,000 people from 1987 to 1995 found those who pray and attend religious services more than once a week have a seven-year longer life expectancy than those who never attend services.

The Faith Factor

This phenomenon might help explain why Jesus frequently said to those He healed, "Your faith has made you well. Go in peace, and be healed of your affliction" (Mark 5:34, NKJV). Indeed, if a person's faith in doctors and drugs can have such a profound influence on our health, how much more powerful would faith in God be on our physical and spiritual well-being?

Jesus said, "If you can believe, all things are possible to him who believes" (Mark 9:23, NKJV). The phenomenal thing about these "faith factor" studies is that when the patients and physicians both believed the patient would get better, healing occurred more frequently. According to one study: "Patients suffering pain after wisdom-tooth extraction got just as much relief from a fake application of ultrasound as from a real one, so long as both patient and therapist thought the machine was on." Perhaps this is related to the truth that collective prayer for an individual's healing has demonstrated real results.

The Social Factor: Healthy People Need People

From the beginning, God created human beings to be social creatures. We have been prewired with a need for healthy, trusting relationships.

Have you ever looked closely at the Ten Commandments? You'll find the first four deal with our relationship with God, while the final six help us to have a trusting relationship with our fellow human beings. This is why Jesus summarized the Decalogue with these two great commandments: to love God and to love our neighbor (Matthew 22:37-40).

Amazingly, modern studies reveal that many health problems can be traced to a breakdown in trust between people. But even more important, trust in God has become increasingly recognized by medicine for its healing influence.

That's why it is so sad that we are now living in a world in which divorce is as common as changing tires, and lonely people sequester themselves in towering concrete cubicles. The television has become a constant companion, while pithy text messaging has replaced a meaningful visit with neighbors.

Recently many secular scientists have come to realize the negative health impact that a collapse in social structures can have. A world-renowned cardiologist, Dean Ornish, had this to say when speaking about the underlying causes of heart disease:

"The real epidemic in our culture is not only physical heart disease, but . . . spiritual heart disease—that is, the profound feelings of loneliness, isolation, alienation, and depression that are so prevalent in our culture with the breakdown of the social structures that used to provide us with a sense of connection and community."

"The Lord God said, It is not good that man should be alone" *(Genesis 2:18, NKJV).*

AMAZING HEALTH **FACTS**

A recent study finds that people who have never married have the highest risk of premature death in the United States. In addition, people who are divorced or separated are 27 percent more likely to die early. Moreover, married men are half as likely to commit suicide as single men, and one third as likely as divorced men. As you can see, social isolation plays a role in mortality.

The social structures that historically connect us with God and community are the church and the family, both introduced in Genesis! Here are some well-known benefits for those who trust in God and fellowship with others through regular church attendance:

- Lower death rates than nonchurchgoers—regardless of risk factors
- Fewer symptoms and better health outcomes in seven of eight cancer studies, four of five blood pressure studies, four of six heart disease studies, and four of five general health studies
- Less vulnerability to depression, suicide, alcoholism, and other addictions
- A 53 percent quicker recovery from depression
- Three times more likely to survive open-heart surgery
- Hospital stays more than two times shorter than older patients without a religious affiliation
- Stronger immune system function

Faith Plus Community

Think the above facts can be explained by social support alone? According to the researchers, social support could account for only 15 percent of the effect. In another study involving two groups living in kibbutzim (Jewish commune) in Israel, one secular, one religious, persons living in religious kibbutzim had less illness and a 50 percent lower mortality rate than those living in even tightly knit secular kibbutzim!

So trusting in God does make a big difference!

Conversely, living without faith in God can also cause a negative impact on health. For two years 444 older patients were followed after their discharge from the hospital. When surveyed, those who wondered "whether or not God had abandoned them" or "if He loved them" had a 20 to 30 percent increase in early mortality as compared to those who had a strong trust in God's love.

So compelling is the evidence for the "faith factor" that even prestigious medical journals such as the *Archives of Internal Medicine* have developed

spiritual questionnaires to assess a patient's level of trust in God. Science indeed has recognized what every person of faith has known intuitively for centuries—trusting God can be very beneficial to your health!

Finding Health in Faith

You might be thinking, "I'm open to being involved in spiritual things and in church, but amid the vast kaleidoscope of religions and denominations to choose from, do some have teachings that are more helpful to health and longevity than others?"

The answer is a resounding yes! Studies indicate that churches that have a high regard for Bible health principles found in the Old and New Testaments do the best in these areas.

No wonder the Bible says, "My son, forget not my law; but let thine heart keep my commandments: for length of days, and long life, and peace, shall they add to thee" (Proverbs 3:1, 2). And, "The fear of the Lord is the beginning of wisdom: and the knowledge of the holy is understanding. For by me thy days shall be multiplied, and the years of thy life shall be increased" (Proverbs 9:10, 11).

Never-ending Health

The most wonderful news of all is that the biblical benefits of a longer, stronger life need not end with a funeral. While the Scriptures declare that "the wages of sin is death," God earnestly desires to offer you forgiveness and a gift of "eternal life" (Romans 6:23).

That life without end can begin for you right now and will continue forever in a world where there is no more sickness, pain, or death (Revelation 21:4).

Two thousand years ago God's Son came to earth as a man. He spent His life healing, feeding, and teaching others how they could have eternal life. He perfectly demonstrated the love of God in His life and taught people how to love each other.

His name was Jesus.

Because He was a threat to the religious and political establishment, He was arrested. After a hasty, irregular trial, He was beaten and crucified. Though innocent, Jesus willingly suffered and died to take the punishment for the sins of all humanity. Whoever believes in the life and sacrifice of God's Son can have all their sins forgiven and receive the gift of everlasting life.

Do you want this gift of eternal life and health? You can receive it right now. Wherever you are reading these words, eternal life can begin for you this moment. All you have to do right now is start by accepting God's amazing gift and believing in the mission of His Son.

If so, say a simple prayer such as the following:

Dear Lord, I thank You for Your wonderful offer of forgiveness and eternal salvation. I freely admit that I've sinned, that I've done things that have hurt You, others, and my own body and mind. I ask that You would forgive me of these sins and that You would cleanse me and give me a new heart and the

gift of eternal life. I want to live my life according to Your words and will. I am now putting my faith in You. Thank You for offering Your Son, Jesus, to take the penalty for all my sins and hearing and answering this prayer. In His name I pray. Amen.

Now that you have accepted Christ, you are like a newborn beginning a new spiritual life with Him. Here is the advice that Scripture gives to those who have just accepted Jesus: "As newborn babes, desire the pure milk of the word, that you may grow thereby" (1 Peter 2:2, NKJV).

Would you like to continue learning how to improve your physical and spiritual health—and live a longer, stronger life? Then take the next step and sign up now for absolutely FREE Bible lessons that will take you even deeper into the incredible life-giving wonders of God's Word.

Just turn to page 127 to get the details on how to take advantage of this FREE offer today!

Special Ingredients

Sometimes plant based vegetarian cookery calls for ingredients with which the average cook might not be familiar. Every attempt has been made to keep such special ingredients to a minimum, but a few are required. Listed below are some of these unique items included in **The Amazing Health Cookbook** recipes. Natural foods are available in the natural foods section of grocery stores, from health food stores and from online vendors.

Almond Butter—A nut butter like peanut butter, but made with roasted almonds.

Bakon Yeast—Similar to nutritional yeast flakes, Bakon yeast is torula yeast with a natural hickory smoke flavor. Gives a wonderful "real southern" flavor to cooked greens.

Bragg Liquid Aminos—This unfermented alternative to soy sauce is lower in sodium and has a mild, delicious, and somewhat "meaty" flavor.

Carob Powder—While there might be validity to deriving some health benefit from dark chocolate, the amount of fat and sugar needed to make it palatable nearly, if not completely, cancels it out. Possessing a flavor and appearance similar to chocolate, carob is actually a legume that is naturally sweet and thus requires less added sweetener. My experience with carob is that "it all depends on the recipe," and those presented in **The Amazing Health Cookbook** have passed many taste tests!

Carob Chips—Similar to chocolate chips, these tasty little morsels are made with carob powder and consequently require less sweetener

than their look-alike. They do contain saturated fat, however, and could be replaced in any recipe with raisins for a healthier alternative.

Cashews—Cashews are soft and blend easily with water into a smooth cream. They should be purchased raw for cooking, whole or in pieces, and rinsed thoroughly as they can contain impurities.

Chicken-style Seasoning—A savory seasoning that gives gravies, tofu, or Soy Curls a delicious chicken-like flavor. McKay's Chicken-Style Seasoning is available commercially, but this recipe is easy to mix and keeps well:

1	cup nutritional yeast flakes
1	tablespoon onion powder
2¼	teaspoons paprika
1½	teaspoons celery seed
1	tablespoon salt
1½	teaspoons sage
1½	teaspoons thyme
1½	teaspoons garlic powder
¾	teaspoon marjoram
1	tablespoon parsley flakes
1	tablespoon turbinado sugar

Combine all ingredients and mix in dry blender. Store in a closed container.

Chili Powder—Hot chilies are irritating to the digestive tract. This "No Alarm" Chili Powder recipe is a healthy alternative to regular chili powder. An occasional dash of cayenne can be used for those who prefer a hotter chili, but it should be used in extreme moderation.

8	bay leaves
½	cup paprika
¼	cup parsley flakes
1	teaspoon garlic powder
1½	tablespoons onion powder

1½	tablespoons sweet basil
4	tablespoons oregano leaves
1½	teaspoons cumin

Blend all ingredients in a dry blender, being sure to blend bay leaves well. Store in airtight container.

Coconut Milk—Studies now show that coconut oil may aid in lowering cholesterol and in normalizing thyroid function, so coconut milk may also be helpful. All my recipes that use this ingredient call not for the lite variety, but for the full-fat canned coconut milk, which produces incredible flavor and texture.

Curry Powder, Mild—A combination of a number of herbs and spices, curry powder is usually quite hot. Here's a recipe you can keep on hand that adds a pungent flavor without the hot, harsh spices.

1	tablespoon coriander
2	teaspoons cumin
2	tablespoons celery seed
1	teaspoon garlic powder
1½	tablespoons turmeric
½	teaspoon ground cardamom
1	tablespoon onion powder
12	bay leaves (optional)

Grind all ingredients in coffee mill or dry blender. If using bay leaves, be sure all leaf fragments are ground very fine. If omitting this ingredient, the curry powder may be mixed in a bowl with a spoon.

Date Sugar—Dried dates are crushed to produce this granulated form of dates. Though an expensive alternative to refined sugar, it is a very tasty whole-food sweetener.

Dulse—A seaweed product that is low in sodium and rich in trace minerals, granulated dulse is very palatable and an excellent alternative to salt, especially when sprinkled on vegetables. It does have a slight fishy taste, so experiment and use it sparingly at first.

Ener-G Baking Powder—Conventional baking powder (sodium bicarbonate and tartaric acid) is high in sodium, robs B vitamins when assimilated, is irritating to the digestive tract, might contribute to the formation of gallstones, and often contains aluminum. While Rumford baking powder is aluminum-free, it still has all the risk factors of other brands. Ener-G baking powder is a combination of citric acid and calcium carbonate, and when used in baking, produces the most readily absorbed form of calcium, calcium citrate. It is moisture activated and requires about double the amount of regular baking powder. Ener-G baking products are available in health food stores, at Adventist Book and Health Food stores at (800) 765-6955, or can be ordered from Ener-G Foods, Inc. at (800) 331-5222 or **www.ener-g.com**

Instant Clear Jel—Also known as modified food starch, this pre-cooked cornstarch instantly thickens puddings and salad dressings when sprinkled into swirling liquid in a running blender.

Lemon Juice—Fresh is always best, but a convenient alternative is pure, reconstituted lemon juice that can be found in the freezer section.

Nutritional Yeast Flakes—Loaded with B vitamins, nutritional yeast flakes give a cheesy flavor and a nutritional boost to dairy-free cheese recipes.

Real Salt—This is the brand name of a product that is 98 percent sodium chloride, but it also contains 50 trace minerals including calcium, potassium, sulphur, phosphorus, manganese, copper, iodine, and zinc. Real Salt is recommended for all recipes that call for salt.

Roma—This roasted grain beverage resembles coffee, but contains no caffeine or tannin. A key ingredient in carob recipes and a delicious warm beverage on a cold winter's night.

Soy Curls—A whole soybean meat substitute, Soy Curls are as versatile as chicken and beef. Included in **The Amazing Health Cookbook** are a number of delicious recipes, but with a little creativity, an endless number of recipes could be developed. Available from Butler Foods at (503) 879-5005, at www.totalvegetarian.com, and some natural foods markets.

Stevia—A no-carbohydrate herbal sweetener that is much sweeter than sugar and provides a healthy alternative. I encourage you to experiment using half-refined sweetener and a small amount of stevia in puddings and whipped topping. SweetLeaf Stevia Plus is the brand I recommend.

Sucanat—The name for this dehydrated sugar cane juice is derived from "sugar cane natural." A simple carbohydrate, Sucanat does have slightly more nutritive value than white or turbinado sugar.

Tahini—A purée of sesame seeds, tahini is a seed butter similar to nut butters such as peanut and almond butter. Its slightly bitter taste makes a perfect ingredient for mock cheese recipes, adding a sharp cheese flavor.

Tofu—Studies have demonstrated that including tofu in the diet might help prevent heart disease, osteoporosis, and breast and prostate cancer and can reduce menopausal symptoms such as mood swings and hot flashes. Low in fat and cholesterol-free, tofu can also contribute significantly to an effective weight-loss program. Providing high-quality protein, tofu, like soybeans, contains isoflavones, including a powerful anti-cancer agent called genestein, as well as other phytochemicals.

Somewhat like cottage cheese, tofu, which is soybean curd, comes in different degrees of firmness. Most of my recipes call for fresh, water-packed firm or extra-firm tofu, since this consistency contains less water and more nutrition. Silken tofu, which comes in an aseptic box, is perfect for puddings or mousse.

Though recognized by many as a "super food," tofu often receives a reluctant reception. Many have had an unfortunate introduction to tofu, and it is my mission to help people recover from their "tofu phobia"! The health benefits and ease of prep-aration of this convenient, nutrient-dense food make it way too good to write off as weird or unsavory. With the recipes you find in **The Amazing Health Cookbook**, I believe you'll find that tofu can be incredibly delicious!

Turbinado Sugar—Also known as raw sugar, turbinado has just a few nutrients, but it provides all the simple carbohydrate grams of regular granulated sugar.

Vegeburger—Available canned or frozen, this crumbled hamburger substitute is made from soy protein or wheat gluten.

Vegenaise—A soy-based, vegan mayonnaise that contains vinegar and lemon juice. Homemade Tofu Mayonnaise contains no vinegar and would be preferable, but Vegenaise can be used for the sake of convenience.

Vegesal—A blend of salt and vegetable crystals with a bit of kelp added, Vegesal is much lower in sodium than table salt. One teaspoon contains 1,420 milligrams of sodium, compared to 2,400 milligrams in salt, which includes sea salt. Real Salt and Herbemare are also recommended.

Carrot Juice

Supplementing your diet with fresh vegetable juices is an excellent way to give yourself a nutritional boost. Juicing carrots and other vegetables produces a beverage that tastes great and is chock-full of vitamins and minerals. Here's one time to be sure to use organically grown produce. Although carrot juice is full of nutrients, including naturally occurring sugar, if conventionally grown produce is used, you'll also get a concentration of pesticides. So, go organic!

INGREDIENTS

1	pound	organically grown carrots

PER 8 OUNCES	
CALORIES	95
PROTEIN	2.2 g
CARBOHYDRATES	22 g
FIBER	1 g
FAT	.3 g
SODIUM	70 mg

STEPS

1 Scrub carrots well. Cut off tops.

2 Extract juice from carrots using a Champion Juicer or another type of juice extractor. Strain and drink immediately. For optimal digestion, swish the juice in your mouth as you drink it.

MAKES ABOUT 1 CUP

Raspberry Zinger Punch

A refreshing beverage that is pretty in the glass and not too sweet. Perfect for wedding receptions!

INGREDIENTS

3	quarts	water
8		Red Zinger tea bags
12-oz can		raspberry white grape juice concentrate

PER 8 OUNCES	
CALORIES	60
PROTEIN	.5 g
CARBOHYDRATES	14 g
FIBER	0 g
FAT	0 g
SODIUM	4 mg

STEPS

1 Bring 1 quart of water to a boil. Add tea bags and let it steep for 5 minutes.

2 Add juice concentrate and remaining 2 quarts of water and stir.

3 Chill and serve with orange slices floating in a punch bowl or with juice and orange slices frozen in gelatin molds afloat.

MAKES 13 SERVINGS

COOK'S TIP

If a lack of refrigerator space makes chilling the punch a challenge, use only 2½ quarts of water, then add a tray of ice cubes just before serving.

Soymilk

Soymilk is available in almost every grocery store these days, with options of plain, vanilla, and unsweetened—even carob and chocolate! Yet homemade soymilk is even more nutritious in that you can choose to keep the fiber and control the amount and type of sweetener used. Additionally, commercial soymilk can cost as much as $.50 per serving, while the homemade version will cost only a dime per serving!

INGREDIENTS

½	cup	dry soybeans
3–4		pitted dates
		water
¼	tsp	salt

COOK'S TIP

Soybeans can be soaked ahead of time and stored in the freezer in plastic bags in 1-cup portions. Rinse them with hot water and proceed with the recipe.

STEPS

1. Cover soybeans in a medium-sized bowl with 2 cups water. Soak overnight or at least five hours. Drain and place in a large saucepan with the dates and 2 cups fresh water.

2. Bring to a boil and allow it to boil gently for 5 minutes.

3. Drain and combine with 2 cups fresh water, dates, and salt. Blend until smooth.

4. Add water or ice cubes to make one quart or to desired consistency. One tray of ice is equal to 2 cups of water. Strain if desired.

MAKES 1 QUART

PER 1 CUP	
CALORIES	99
PROTEIN	8.5 g
CARBOHYDRATES	8 g
FIBER	3.3 g
FAT	4.5 g
SODIUM	76 mg

Green Smoothie

Absolutely the best way to get your calcium and other important minerals.

INGREDIENTS

2	cups	fresh pineapple chunks
2	cups	fresh parsley, packed
½	cup	water
4		ice cubes
		sprinkle of stevia powder
2	tbsp	pineapple juice concentrate (optional)

STEPS

1. Include the core of the pineapple when preparing it for the smoothie.

2. Combine all ingredients in blender and blend until smooth.

MAKES 3 CUPS

PER CUP	
CALORIES	50
PROTEIN	1.7 g
CARBOHYDRATES	12.5 g
FIBER	2.5 g
FAT	0 g
SODIUM	25 mg

COOK'S TIP

You also can use kale, spinach, or young collards for this mineral-rich drink. Better yet, use lambsquarters, often considered a weed, right out of your yard or garden.

Cappuccino

With this easy recipe, you can skip the coffee and have the added benefit of soymilk. Enjoy a small serving with dessert.

INGREDIENTS

2	cups	vanilla soymilk
2	tbsp	maple syrup
2	tsp	powdered coffee substitute (Roma *or* Pero)
½	tsp	vanilla extract

PER ½ CUP	
CALORIES	60
PROTEIN	4.5 g
CARBOHYDRATES	12.5 g
FIBER	1.5 g
FAT	2.5 g
SODIUM	15 mg

STEPS

1 Briefly blend all ingredients in a blender.

2 Serve hot or chilled.

MAKES 4 SERVINGS

"You must take time for your health, or you will take time for disease."—AGATHA THRASH, M.D.

Sweet Nut Milk

There's no need for sugary cereals with this delicious nut milk poured over granola and other wholesome cereals.

INGREDIENTS

1	quart	water
⅔	cup	rinsed, raw cashews *or* almonds
4		pitted dates
¼	tsp	salt
½	tsp	lemon juice

PER ½ CUP	
CALORIES	105 g
PROTEIN	3.1 g
CARBOHYDRATES	7.3 g
FIBER	.8 g
FAT	7.4 g
SODIUM	69 mg

STEPS

1 Place nuts, dates, and salt in blender with 1 cup of the water and blend until smooth. Add remaining water and blend again to mix.

2 Serve immediately with hot cereal. Otherwise, store in the refrigerator for later use.

3 Shake well before each use.

MAKES 4½ CUPS

COOK'S TIP

For "unsweetened" nut milk, decrease sweetener to one date or ½ teaspoon of honey. Milk from dairy is not exactly sweet, but its flavor is not flat either. The taste of milk is actually a combination of three tastes: sweet, sour, and salty. That's why even this "unsweetened" nut milk requires a small amount of sweetener to achieve the desired flavor.

Tropical Milk

Cow's milk is the perfect food for baby cows! Dairy milk is linked to many diseases in humans, from juvenile diabetes and allergies to digestive problems and degenerative diseases. This alternative is delicious.

INGREDIENTS

13.5-oz can	coconut milk
1	tbsp	sweetener
½	tsp	vanilla extract
⅛	tsp	salt
		water to make 2 quarts

STEPS

1 Combine all ingredients in half gallon jar. Fill with water. Add part ice cubes if chilling the milk immediately is desired.

2 Store in refrigerator.

MAKES 16 SERVINGS

PER ½ CUP	
CALORIES	50
PROTEIN	.5 g
CARBOHYDRATES	1.5 g
FIBER	0 g
FAT	5 g
SODIUM	45 mg

Hot Carob

Nothing beats a hot drink like this one on a chilly evening. Gather around the fire and enjoy a cup!

INGREDIENTS

2	cups	vanilla soymilk
1½	tsp	carob powder
1	tbsp	honey
¼	tsp	stevia powder
½	tsp	vanilla extract
		dash of salt

STEPS

1 Briefly blend all ingredients in a blender.

2 Heat in a saucepan over medium heat, just until steaming.

3 Serve hot.

MAKES 2 SERVINGS

PER 8 OUNCES	
CALORIES	165
PROTEIN	9.5 g
CARBOHYDRATES	23 g
FIBER	3.5 g
FAT	5 g
SODIUM	110 mg

Scrambled Tofu

Serve **Oven Roasted Potatoes,** *page 97*, **Scrambled Tofu,** and sliced tomatoes for a savory breakfast treat that provides a great nutritional foundation for a productive day!

INGREDIENTS

1	tsp	salt
1	tbsp	parsley flakes *or* chopped fresh parsley
14	oz.	fresh, firm tofu
¼	cup	rinsed, raw cashews
2	tbsp	nutritional yeast flakes
⅛	tsp	turmeric *or*
2	tbsp	cooked carrots
¼	tsp	garlic powder
½	tsp	lemon juice
2	tsp	onion powder
½	cup	water

STEPS

1. Crumble tofu into fine pieces in a nonstick skillet. A potato masher works well for this. Sprinkle with parsley and ¼ teaspoon of the salt. Heat in the skillet about 10 minutes until dry.

2. Blend the remaining ingredients, including the remaining ¾ teaspoon of salt, in a blender until smooth. Pour the blended mixture over tofu in skillet and scramble over medium heat until desired consistency.

MAKES 4 SERVINGS

PER ½ CUP	
CALORIES	240
PROTEIN	19.9 g
CARBOHYDRATES	10.8 g
FIBER	4.1 g
FAT	15.4 g
SODIUM	600 mg

Overnight Waffles

A hearty meal disguised as a waffle breakfast

INGREDIENTS

¾	cup	dry soybeans
½	cup	brown rice
2		pitted dates
½	cup	cornmeal
¾	tsp	salt
1	tsp	vanilla
2½	cups	water

STEPS

1. Cover dry soybeans, rice, and dates with 4 cups water in a large bowl. Allow to soak overnight and drain water. They will approximately double in size.

2. Combine soybeans, rice, and dates and place in blender with remaining ingredients.

3. Blend until smooth.

4. Bake in preheated oil-sprayed waffle iron, 8-9 minutes.

5. Serve with fresh peaches or strawberries and **Berry Fruit Sauce,** *page 112*.

MAKES 12 PANCAKES

> ### COOK'S TIP
> The thinner the batter, the lighter the waffle. Experiment and adjust the water according to your preference.

PER PANCAKE	
CALORIES	200
PROTEIN	10.5 g
CARBOHYDRATES	29 g
FIBER	4 g
FAT	5.5 g
SODIUM	290 mg

Stoplight Tofu

Red, yellow, and green bell peppers are often sold together. One package I saw was cylindrical and looked like a traffic light! These peppers are chock-full of vitamin C and add an appealing array of color. This breakfast recipe is sure to give you the green light for a great day!

INGREDIENTS

1		small onion
½		green bell pepper
½		yellow bell pepper
½		red bell pepper
14	ounces	fresh, firm tofu
2	tsp	chicken-style seasoning
¼	tsp	turmeric
1½	tsp	olive oil *or*
1	tbsp	water
2	tsp	parsley flakes
		salt to taste

STEPS

1. Peel and slice onion in half, then into thin slices. Cut peppers into 2" x ½" strips; slice tofu into ¼" x 1" squares.

2. Sauté onions and peppers in oil or steam in water for 3 minutes.

3. Add tofu and seasonings and stir to coat. Cover and steam for 5 more minutes.

MAKES 4 SERVINGS

PER 1 CUP	
CALORIES	185
PROTEIN	16.5 g
CARBOHYDRATES	11 g
FIBER	3.5 g
FAT	10 g
SODIUM	565 mg

Stuffed French Toast

A great take-along breakfast, these pitas resemble a fruit pie after baking. Our vacations always started early in the morning with a breakfast on the road of **Stuffed French Toast,** dipped into individual cups of **Strawberry Jam.**

HEALTH TIP

An abundance of valuable fiber is found not only in whole grains, but also in fruits, vegetables, and legumes.

INGREDIENTS

¼	cup	pitted dates
½	cup	raw cashews
2	tbsp	rolled oats
1	cup	water
¼	tsp	salt (*or* less)
4		whole-wheat pitas
13.5-oz can		pears, in juice

STEPS

1. Blend dates, cashews, salt, and water until very smooth and pour into a shallow dish.

2. Cut pita bread in half. Stuff with pears, flattening the pears as you stuff them into the pita pocket, and bring the opening of the pita back together as much as possible. Dip bread into batter, carefully covering the top well, not leaving fingerprints!

3. Bake on baking sheet, ideally covered with parchment paper at 350°F for 30 minutes.

4. Serve with **Berry Fruit Sauce,** *page 112,* or **Strawberry Jam,** *page 113.*

MAKES 8 SERVINGS

PER SERVING	
CALORIES	160
PROTEIN	4.5 g
CARBOHYDRATES	22 g
FIBER	3 g
FAT	7 g
SODIUM	100 mg

French Toast

The original recipe called for stale bread. In fact, the French, who apparently developed the recipe, call it "pain perdu" or "lost bread," bread that would otherwise be lost! But mercy intervenes and nothing is lost in this recipe, except the unwanted cholesterol.

INGREDIENTS

¼	cup	pitted dates
½	cup	rinsed, raw cashews
1	cup	water
¼	tsp	salt (or less)
8	slices	**Whole-Wheat Bread**, *page 55*

STEPS

1 In the blender, blend dates, cashews, salt, and water until very smooth. Pour into a shallow dish and dip bread into batter.

2 Brown in a preheated, nonstick skillet over medium heat, or bake on a baking sheet at 350°F for 30 minutes.

3 Serve with **Berry Fruit Sauce**, *page 112*, or simply with applesauce or fresh fruit. Delicious with peaches served on top!

MAKES 8 SLICES

PER SLICE	
CALORIES	160
PROTEIN	5 g
CARBOHYDRATES	20 g
FIBER	3 g
FAT	8 g
SODIUM	210 mg

Fancy Crockpot Cereal

HEALTH TIP

For best digestion and assimilation of nutrients, eat fruit at one meal and vegetables at another.

More taste, more nutrition, wonderful texture. If it's your turn to fix breakfast, do it in five minutes the night before!

INGREDIENTS

⅓	cup	wheat berries
⅓	cup	oat groats *or rolled oats*
⅓	cup	quinoa *or millet*
½	cup	applesauce
¼	cup	shredded coconut
½	tsp	salt
1	tsp	coriander
¼	cup	chopped dried pineapple (optional)
3½	cups	water

STEPS

1 Combine all ingredients in a 1-quart crockpot and cook on low overnight.

2 Toss in a few raisins in the morning, if desired.

3 Serve with fresh fruit, granola, and soy or nut milk.

MAKES 4 SERVINGS

PER CUP (WITHOUT DRIED PINEAPPLE AND RAISINS)	
CALORIES	160
PROTEIN	4 g
CARBOHYDRATES	30 g
FIBER	3.4 g
FAT	3.4 g
SODIUM	300 mg

Belgian Waffles

You won't have to call anyone to breakfast twice after the aroma of these waffles wafts through the house. You will be amazed how light and golden brown with crispy edges these are, without eggs or baking powder. The heat of the waffle iron does the leavening.

COOK'S TIP

Use a regular waffle iron for thinner waffles. Waffles can be made ahead of time and frozen for later use. Just pop them in the toaster!

INGREDIENTS

4 ¾	cups	water
¾	tsp	salt
¼	cup	nuts *or* seeds
½	cup	cornmeal
⅛	cup	date pieces
3	cups	rolled oats

Variation: For sesame oat waffles, sprinkle waffle iron with 1 teaspoon sesame seeds, pour batter and sprinkle top with sesame seeds before baking.

STEPS

1. Blend all ingredients except the oats, starting with 2 cups of water.

2. Add oats and 2¼ cups of the remaining water and blend until smooth. Let the batter sit for 3 minutes.

3. Pour 1¼ cups of batter onto preheated, oil-sprayed Belgian waffle iron, not allowing batter to come completely to sides. Bake for 10 to 12 minutes or until golden brown.

4. Add another ¼ cup of the water to batter and blend again. You will see batter thickens as it sits. Pour the second waffle in the iron, then add the final ¼ cup of water and blend again. Repeat process. Waffle iron may get hotter during the process, so watch carefully! Cooking time might need to be decreased.

MAKES 6 WAFFLES

PER WAFFLE	
CALORIES	330
PROTEIN	12 g
CARBOHYDRATES	42 g
FIBER	7.5 g
FAT	14 g
SODIUM	300 mg

Hi-Fiber Granola

Granola adds a wonderful crunch to hot cereal. Bake this overnight in a "slow" oven and breakfast will be ready when you wake up in the morning. The aroma will let you know!

COOK'S TIP

Bananas that have been frozen and thawed work well in this recipe. Keep some on hand in the freezer for granola and for smoothies!

INGREDIENTS

2		ripe bananas
1	cup	pitted dates
¾	cup	water
6	cups	old-fashioned rolled oats
1	cup	wheat bran
½	cup	ground flaxseed
1¼	tsp	salt
1	cup	chopped walnuts
1	cup	chipped coconut

STEPS

1. Heat dates and water together. Blend until smooth in blender with bananas and salt.

2. Combine remaining ingredients in a large bowl. Add blended mixture and, using plastic gloves, mix well with hands. It should stick together when grabbed by the handful.

3. Bake on two nonstick cookie sheets in the oven overnight at 170°F, with the oven setting on "warm." In the morning, raise oven temperature to 200°F for 30 minutes to brown slightly.

4. Serve over fruit or **Crockpot Cereal**, *page 50*, and add soy or nut milk, or use as a topping for pudding or banana smoothies.

MAKES 24 SERVINGS

PER ½ CUP	
CALORIES	180
PROTEIN	5 g
CARBOHYDRATES	25.5 g
FIBER	4.2 g
FAT	7 g
SODIUM	140 mg

Maple Walnut Granola

Rich but delicious, a little of this granola goes a long way. A great topping for pudding or smoothies.

INGREDIENTS

1	cup	pitted dates
¾	cup	water
½	cup	maple syrup
¼	cup	light olive oil
2	tsp	vanilla extract
2	tsp	maple extract
1½	tsp	salt
7	cups	old-fashioned rolled oats
1	cup	unsweetened chipped coconut
1	cup	walnuts, coarsely chopped
1	cup	pecan meal
1	cup	pumpkin *or* sunflower seeds

PER ½ CUP	
CALORIES	245
PROTEIN	9 g
CARBOHYDRATES	32 g
FIBER	3 g
FAT	10 g
SODIUM	130 mg

STEPS

1 Heat dates and water in the microwave or in a saucepan until dates are soft. Place in the blender with maple syrup, oil, vanilla and maple extracts, and salt. Blend until smooth.

2 In a large bowl, combine all dry ingredients and pour in the blended mixture. Using plastic gloves, mix with your hands until the dry ingredients are well coated. Mixture should hold together when you squeeze a handful together.

3 Spread out on two cookie sheets covered with parchment paper or sprayed with oil.

4 Bake overnight at 125°F, with the oven setting on "warm," or for 2 hours at 225°F, stirring every 30 minutes.

MAKES 27 SERVINGS

HEALTH TIP

The high selenium content of Brazil nuts discourages the aging process! In just one ounce of these potassium-rich nuts, there are 840 micrograms of selenium. Replace walnuts with chopped Brazil nuts in granola from time to time and enjoy the benefits.

Charlie's Cran-Apple Granola

A love of certain ingredients can be the inspiration for a great recipe. That was true in Charlie's case; she's crazy about Craisins! And her recipe has gotten rave reviews.

INGREDIENTS

7	cups	quick oats
1	cup	sliced almonds
1	cup	chopped dried apples
1	cup	dried cranberries
1		banana
1	cup	pitted dates
⅓	cup	Sucanat *or* turbinado sugar
¼	cup	light olive oil
1	tbsp	vanilla extract
¾	cup	water
1½	tsp	salt

STEPS

1. Place dry ingredients in a large bowl.
2. Blend banana, dates, sugar, oil, vanilla, water, and salt in blender until smooth and pour over dry ingredients.
3. Using a plastic glove, mix both mixtures together with your hands. When thoroughly mixed, spread out on two cookie sheets covered with parchment paper or oil-sprayed.
4. Bake at 170°F, with the oven setting on "warm," overnight or for two hours at 225°F, stirring every 30 minutes. Store in airtight container.

MAKES 24 SERVINGS

PER ½ CUP	
CALORIES	202
PROTEIN	5 g
CARBOHYDRATES	33.6 g
FIBER	3.9 g
FAT	6.3 g
SODIUM	151 mg

"His compassions fail not. They are new every morning; great is Your faithfulness."—LAMENTATIONS 3:22, 23, NKJV

Baked Oatmeal

This no-fuss recipe can be made the night before and baked just before breakfast. I like to add a cup of blueberries for a fruity punch of antioxidants!

INGREDIENTS

3	cups	rolled oats
¾	cup	raisins or chopped dates
½	cup	coconut, unsweetened
1	tsp	salt
4½	cups	water

STEPS

1. Mix all ingredients in oil-sprayed 13" x 9" pan.
2. Bake uncovered at 350°F for about 1 hour.

MAKES 12 SERVINGS

COOK'S TIP
To decrease baking time, use hot water in this recipe.

PER ½ CUP	
CALORIES	170
PROTEIN	4.2 g
CARBOHYDRATES	24 g
FIBER	4 g
FAT	7.4 g
SODIUM	200 mg

Honey Wheat Bread

Made by hand or in a bread machine, this recipe seems to be foolproof. The molasses makes all the difference!

INGREDIENTS

1¼	cups	warm water
1	tbsp	honey
1	tbsp	molasses
2	tsp	dry yeast*
1	tsp	salt
1½	tbsp	oil
1½	cups	unbleached white flour
1½	cups	whole-wheat flour
¼	cup	additional flour for kneading

If using a bread machine, decrease yeast to 1¼ teaspoons.

STEPS

1. Put the warm water in a large mixing bowl. Add the honey and molasses and stir until they are dissolved.

2. Sprinkle in the yeast and stir. Let this mixture rest until the yeast comes to the top of the mixture, a matter of only two or three minutes. This step is to "proof" the yeast, making sure it has leavening power.

3. Add the salt and the oil and stir, making sure that all ingredients are mixed well. Add half of the flour and beat the batter for 3 to 5 minutes.

4. Add the rest of the flour gradually. You need less on a dry day, more on a damp day. Use an extra ¼ cup flour if it is needed to absorb the liquid in forming a ball of dough.

5. Place the dough ball on a surface sprinkled with flour. Rub a little flour on your hands and proceed to knead. Fold the dough toward you. Using the heels of your hands, push the dough away from you with a rolling motion. Do not be afraid to use a firm touch. Swing the dough a quarter turn around.

6. Repeat the kneading technique until the dough is smooth and elastic, 8 to 10 minutes. If the dough becomes sticky, sprinkle the surface with a small amount of flour and rub your hands with flour again. The dough has been kneaded enough when it is pressed with a finger and it springs back.

7. Place the ball of dough in a large oiled mixing bowl and cover it with a damp cloth. Let it rise in a warm place, free from draft until it doubles in bulk, about an hour.

8. Test for readiness by pressing the dough carefully with your thumb. If the hole remains, the bread has risen enough.

9. Push your fist into the center of the dough, pull the edges to the center, and turn it over. Cover the dough and let it rest for 15 minutes. This resting encourages development of the gluten, the protein part of the flour.

10. Flatten out the dough. Fold each side to the middle, the width being the length of the bread pan. Start at the top and roll toward you, pressing with each turn to get out the air bubbles, which make the texture of the loaf coarse.

11. Place the formed loaf into an oiled loaf pan, 8½" x 4½" x 2½" in size, with the seam side of the loaf on the bottom of the pan. Cover with a damp cloth and let rise in a warm place free from drafts until it has doubled in bulk, about one hour. The bread is ready for the oven when the dough just begins to go over the edge of the pan.

12. Bake in oven preheated to 350°F for 40 minutes or until brown on the bottom.

13. Remove from pan at once. If the loaf has not browned well on the outside, return it to the oven set on a cookie sheet until browned nicely. Set on wire rack to cool.

MAKES 1 LOAF

PER SLICE, ¹⁄₁₆ OF A LOAF	
CALORIES	99
PROTEIN	3.2 g
CARBOHYDRATES	20.5 g
FIBER	2 g
FAT	.8 g
SODIUM	148 mg

"Jesus said to them, 'I am the bread of life. He who comes to Me shall never hunger, and he who believes in Me shall never thirst.'" — JOHN 6:35, NKJV

Whole-Wheat Bread

100-percent **Whole-Wheat Bread** is a hearty, but flavorful, bread.

INGREDIENTS

4	cups	warm water
⅓	cup	honey
2	tbsp	dry yeast
9-9½ cups		whole-wheat flour*
¼	cup	oil
¼	cup	gluten flour
1	tbsp	salt

STEPS

1. In a large bowl, stir together water, honey, yeast, and 2 cups of the whole-wheat flour; let bubble in warm place 15 to 20 minutes to "proof" the yeast.

2. Stir in oil and salt. Gradually add about 6 cups* of whole-wheat flour until it becomes difficult to stir.

3. Turn dough out onto floured surface and add 1 to 1½ cups more flour. Knead well until texture is correct.

Dough should spring back when lightly pressed.

4. Put the dough back into the bowl, cover, and let it rise in warm place until about double in bulk.

5. Punch down and knead briefly in the bowl. Cut into three equal pieces. Knead each piece on lightly floured counter.

6. Shape into loaves and place in oiled pans, 8½" x 4½" x 2½" in size. Cover and let it rise again in pans in warm place until not quite doubled in size.

7. Bake in oven preheated to 350°F for 40 to 45 minutes. Remove from pans and allow to cool on a wire rack.

8. Allow to "rest" 24 hours so byproducts of yeast fermentation dissipate.

* Flour amount may vary on account of moisture variations in the flour and air.

MAKES 3 LOAVES

COOK'S TIP

The gluten flour adds to the meshwork of the bread dough, allowing it to rise well. Often called "vital gluten," gluten flour is sold in natural foods markets.

PER SLICE	
CALORIES	100
PROTEIN	3.5 g
CARBOHYDRATES	19.5 g
FIBER	3 g
FAT	1.5 g
SODIUM	150 mg

Blueberry Muffins

A nice addition to breakfast or brunch, these muffins are whole grain and contain antioxidant morsels bursting with flavor. Little refined sweetener is needed with the natural sweetness of the pineapple.

INGREDIENTS

¼	cup	almond butter or light olive oil
20-oz can		crushed pineapple with juice
2	tsp	vanilla extract
⅔	cup	honey
2¾	cups	whole wheat pastry flour
½	tsp	salt
3	tbsp	Ener-G baking powder *or*
1½	tbsp	Rumford baking powder
2	cups	blueberries, fresh *or* frozen

STEPS

1. Preheat oven to 375°F.

2. Blend almond butter or oil, pineapple, vanilla extract, and honey in blender until smooth.

3. Combine unsifted flour, salt, and baking powder in a large bowl and mix well.

4. Pour wet mixture into dry ingredients and mix well but quickly, being careful not to stir out bubbles.

5. Fold in blueberries. If berries are frozen, rinse briefly under warm water before adding.

6. Line muffin tin with paper baking cups. Spray the cups with oil to ensure easy removal. Fill muffin cups almost full. Bake for 30 minutes.

MAKES 18 MUFFINS

COOK'S TIP

Pastry flour is made from spring wheat berries and is somewhat finer than regular whole-wheat flour. If only regular whole wheat is available, use 1 cup unbleached white flour and 1½ cups whole wheat.

Variations: Sprinkle with turbinado sugar before baking, or for **Cranberry Muffins,** omit blueberries and add ½ cup chopped walnuts, 1 cup fresh, sliced cranberries, and 1 teaspoon grated orange zest.

PER MUFFIN	
CALORIES	120
PROTEIN	2 g
CARBOHYDRATES	24 g
FIBER	2.5 g
FAT	2 g
SODIUM	60 mg

Cranberry Oat Muffins

Freeze some cranberries when they are available and you won't have to wait until the holidays to serve these muffins. Dense but delicious!

INGREDIENTS

1	cup	drained, crushed pineapple
1		ripe banana, mashed
¼	cup	almond butter
¼	cup	honey
½	tsp	salt
1	tsp	coriander
2	cups	quick oats
¼	cup	chopped walnuts
½	cup	unsweetened coconut
1	cup	date pieces
1	cup	halved, fresh cranberries

STEPS

1. Preheat oven to 350°F.
2. Mix together pineapple, banana, almond butter, and honey in a large bowl.
3. Add remaining ingredients and mix well.
4. Spoon into oil-sprayed muffin tin. Heap mixture into the shape of a muffin, as they do not rise.
5. Bake for 45 minutes.

MAKES 1 DOZEN MUFFINS

PER MUFFIN	
CALORIES	260
PROTEIN	4 g
CARBOHYDRATES	35 g
FIBER	5 g
FAT	12.5 g
SODIUM	130 mg

Soy Corn Muffins

These muffins are served up with black-eyed peas, **Fresh Collard Greens**, *page 98*, and **Sweet Potato Soufflé**, *page 100*, southern style! These muffins are hearty but really delicious.

INGREDIENTS

2	cups	soaked soybeans (1 cup dry)
2	cups	cornmeal, unrefined
2¼	cups	water
1½	tsp	salt
¼	cup	quick oats
2	tbsp	honey
½	tsp	onion powder

PER MUFFIN	
CALORIES	160
PROTEIN	8 g
CARBOHYDRATES	26 g
FIBER	4.5 g
FAT	4 g
SODIUM	290 mg

COOK'S TIP

The soybeans add nutrition and act as a leavening agent, so no eggs or baking powder are needed. Be sure to keep some frozen soaked soybeans on hand so you'll have everything you need for this recipe.

STEPS

1. Preheat oven to 400°F.
2. For 2 cups soaked soybeans, soak 1 cup dry soybeans in 3 cups water overnight or for 5 hours. The beans may be soaked in advance and stored in plastic bags in the freezer.
3. Combine all ingredients except the cornmeal in the blender and blend until smooth. Pour into a bowl and add cornmeal. Mix well.
4. Spoon batter into oiled muffin tin, filling to the top to make 12 muffins. A preheated, oil-sprayed cast iron corn pone pan also works well.
5. Bake for 30 minutes and serve hot. Store any leftover muffins in the refrigerator. Steam to reheat.

MAKES 1 DOZEN

Orange Cranberry Bread

Fruity and festive, this recipe is a colorful addition to holiday fare.

INGREDIENTS

20-oz can		crushed pineapple
1	tbsp	orange zest
¾	cup	orange sections and juice
¼	cup	frozen orange *or* pineapple juice concentrate
¼	cup	honey
¼	cup	tahini *or* light olive oil
1	cup	cranberries
2	cups	whole-wheat flour
1	cup	unbleached white flour
2	tbsp	Ener-G baking powder *or*
1	tbsp	Rumford baking powder
½	tsp	salt
¼	cup	golden raisins
½	cup	chopped walnuts

STEPS

1. Preheat oven to 375°F. Drain some juice from the pineapple so that 1½ cups of pineapple and juice remain.

2. Blend the first six ingredients in a blender until smooth. The orange rind can be in little chunks since the mixture will be blended. Add the cranberries and pulse the blender briefly to chop.

3. Combine flours, baking powder, and salt in a large bowl and mix well. Fold blended mixture into dry ingredients, being careful not to stir out bubbles. Add the walnuts and raisins and stir briefly.

4. Bake in 3 small oil-sprayed loaf pans, approximately 3¼" x 5¾" in size, for 50 minutes. After 10 minutes, reduce oven temperature to 350°F.

MAKES 3 SMALL LOAVES

PER SLICE	
CALORIES	120
PROTEIN	2.5 g
CARBOHYDRATES	28 g
FIBER	2.5 g
FAT	3 g
SODIUM	45 mg

"My Father giveth you the true bread from heaven." — JOHN 6:32

Banana Nut Bread

A breakfast bread that is perfect for a tea or brunch, it bakes to a beautiful golden brown.

INGREDIENTS

½	cup	light olive oil
2	tsp	vanilla extract
1	cup	frozen white grape juice concentrate
1¼	cup	water
1	cup	unbleached flour
2	cups	whole-wheat pastry flour
⅓	cup	date sugar
1½	tsp	stevia powder
1	tsp	salt
2½	tbsp	Ener-G baking powder *or*
1	tbsp	Rumford baking powder
3		medium-ripe bananas, mashed
¾	cup	walnut pieces, coarsely chopped

STEPS

1. Preheat oven to 350°F.

2. Mix wet ingredients in a bowl. Beat with a whisk for 100 strokes or 1 minute with an electric mixer.

3. Dice bananas into ¼-inch pieces. Add bananas and walnuts to wet ingredients.

4. Mix dry ingredients in a separate bowl. Add liquid mixture and mix quickly and well. Pour into two oil-sprayed loaf pans and place directly into the oven.

5. Bake for 45 minutes.

MAKES 16 SLICES OR 18 MUFFINS

PER SLICE	
CALORIES	235
PROTEIN	3.5 g
CARBOHYDRATES	39.5 g
FIBER	2 g
FAT	7.5 g
SODIUM	150 mg

COOK'S TIP

Also makes very nice muffins, which need to bake only 30 to 35 minutes.

Zucchini Muffins

When it comes to a rich source of potassium, zucchini takes the cake. One medium zucchini contains as much potassium as a medium banana, about 450 milligrams.

INGREDIENTS

1	cup	crushed pineapple, with juice
½	cup	light olive oil
¾	cup	Sucanat *or* turbinado sugar
½	cup	soymilk
2	tsp	vanilla
1	tsp	salt
½	tsp	stevia powder*
2	cups	grated zucchini
1	cup	chopped dates
1	cup	walnuts, chopped
2½	cups	whole-wheat pastry flour
2½	tbsp	Ener-G baking powder *or*
1	tbsp	Rumford baking powder
½	tsp	coriander
¼	tsp	cardamom (scant)

STEPS

1. Preheat oven to 350°F.
2. Mix first seven ingredients in a large mixing bowl.
3. Grate zucchini and squeeze out juice. Add zucchini, chopped dates, and walnuts to bowl and mix.
4. Combine flour, baking powder, coriander, and cardamom in a separate bowl. Stir with a whisk to mix.
5. Fold flour mixture into wet ingredients, mixing well. Form muffins in oil-sprayed muffin tin with ice-cream scoop.
6. Bake 40 to 45 minutes until lightly browned.

   *The ½ teaspoon stevia powder may be substituted with 3 tablespoons more Sucanat or turbinado sugar.

MAKES 18 MUFFINS

PER MUFFIN	
CALORIES	225
PROTEIN	4 g
CARBOHYDRATES	31 g
FIBER	3.5 g
FAT	11 g
SODIUM	215 mg

COOK'S TIP

This recipe may also be made as a cake, loaf, or mini-muffins with cooking time adjusted.

Creamy Lemon Dip

A simple fruit platter can be made very special with this yummy dip. In the StepFast Lifestyle Series an introduction to tofu is made via this recipe and the response is always "I can't believe this is tofu!"

INGREDIENTS

12.3 ounces		firm, silken tofu
3	tbsp	lemon juice
½	tsp	lemon extract
⅓	cup +	pineapple juice concentrate
1	tbsp	
2	tbsp	water
¹⁄₁₆	tsp	salt
1	tbsp	light olive oil

STEPS

1 Place all ingredients into blender and blend until smooth.

2 Chill and serve with fresh fruit.

MAKES 1¼ CUPS

PER 2 TABLESPOONS	
CALORIES	50
PROTEIN	3 g
CARBOHYDRATES	4 g
FIBER	.5 g
FAT	2.5 g
SODIUM	10 mg

Sunflower Sour Cream

Although this is somewhat different from sour cream, it makes a good accompaniment to baked potatoes and steamed vegetables. It's also an excellent raw vegetable dip.

INGREDIENTS

½	cup	raw sunflower seeds
½	cup	hot, cooked brown rice
¾	cup	water
¼	tsp	dill weed
1	tsp	salt
1½	tsp	onion powder
½	tsp	garlic powder
⅓	cup	lemon juice

STEPS

1 Combine all ingredients in a blender and blend until smooth.

2 Place in refrigerator to chill.

MAKES 2 CUPS

PER 2 TABLESPOONS	
CALORIES	40
PROTEIN	1.5 g
CARBOHYDRATES	3 g
FIBER	.5 g
FAT	2.3 g
SODIUM	160 mg

Hummus

Originating in the Middle East, this delicious spread transcends almost all cultures and can be used in a variety of ways. One of my favorite things to do with hummus is to put it in a wrap along with lettuce, tomatoes, cucumbers, and olive slices. The sodium content is fairly high but evens out if served with lots of raw veggies. Also, the salt may be decreased if desired.

INGREDIENTS

15.5-oz can	garbanzos, drained
1½ tbsp	lemon juice
2 tbsp	tahini *or* olive oil
½ tsp	garlic powder *or*
1 clove	fresh garlic
½ tsp	salt (scant)
½ cup	water
1 tsp	cumin (optional)

STEPS

1 Blend all ingredients until smooth. Home-cooked garbanzos may be used, adjusting salt to taste according to the salt in garbanzos.

2 Serve with pita bread, with raw veggies, or use as sandwich or wrap filling.

MAKES 1½ CUPS

PER ½ CUP	
CALORIES	215
PROTEIN	5 g
CARBOHYDRATES	22.5 g
FIBER	6.5 g
FAT	10 g
SODIUM	465 mg

Jack Cheese Spread

A delicious, cheesy spread—*sans fromage*—that's "without cheese" in French! Great on sandwiches or with crackers. Makes a great grilled-cheese sandwich!

INGREDIENTS

2 cups	hot cornmeal mush*
¼ cup	tahini
1½ tsp	salt
¼ cup	nutritional yeast flakes
1 tbsp	onion powder
¼ tsp	garlic powder
1 tbsp	lemon juice

To make cornmeal mush, bring 4 cups water to a boil in a medium saucepan. Gradually whisk in 1 cup of cornmeal. Stirring constantly, bring to a boil then reduce heat to simmer, cover and cook for 30 minutes. This may be used as a breakfast "side of grits," or as a hot cereal.

STEPS

1 In blender, whiz all ingredients until smooth. You may need to add another ¼-⅓ cup water, depending on how mushy the cornmeal mush is.

2 Pour mixture into a small serving bowl. Cool well and refrigerate until firm and spreadable.

MAKES 14 SERVINGS

COOK'S TIP

For Jack Cheese Sauce, add ½ cup water. Adjust the salt to taste.

PER ¼ CUP	
CALORIES	75
PROTEIN	2.5 g
CARBOHYDRATES	10 g
FIBER	1.5 g
FAT	3.5 g
SODIUM	415 mg

Salsa

The world seems to be divided into two groups of people: those who love cilantro and those who don't. Both aromatic and therapeutic, cilantro is a key herb in many cuisines and central to salsa, though those who do not care for it can omit it! The lemon juice gives this a wonderful, fresh taste, and this recipe is almost as simple as opening a jar.

INGREDIENTS

1½	cups	chopped tomatoes (fresh or canned)
1	tbsp	lemon juice
1½	tsp	cumin *or* to taste
½	tsp	paprika
2	tsp	onion, chopped small
¼	tsp	salt
1	small	clove of garlic, pressed
1½	tsp	sweet basil
1	tbsp	chopped cilantro

STEPS

1 Combine all ingredients in a blender, then pulse briefly, leaving vegetables chunky.

2 Taste and adjust salt, as it will vary according to the tomatoes used.

MAKES 2 CUPS

PER ¼ CUP	
CALORIES	20
PROTEIN	1 g
CARBOHYDRATES	4 g
FIBER	1 g
FAT	.5 g
SODIUM	150 mg

HEALTH TIP

Avoid heavy or late suppers and you will wake up with a sunny disposition!

Quick & Easy Cheese

More like a dip, this nondairy cheese is perfect on a taco salad, burritos, or **Pita Pizza,** *page 93.* The pimientos may be omitted for a substitute mozzarella on pizza or **Veggie Patch Flatbread,** *page 84.*

INGREDIENTS

12.3 ounces		firm, silken tofu
2½	tbsp	tahini *or* sesame seeds
½	cup	pimientos
½	cup	water
2	tbsp	nutritional yeast flakes
2	tbsp	lemon juice
¾	tsp	salt
1¼	tsp	onion powder
¼	tsp	garlic powder

STEPS

1 Combine all ingredients in a blender and blend until smooth.

2 Serve immediately or chill before serving.

MAKES 15 SERVINGS

PER 3 TABLESPOONS	
CALORIES	55
PROTEIN	4.5 g
CARBOHYDRATES	2.5 g
FIBER	1.5 g
FAT	3.5 g
SODIUM	125 mg

COOK'S TIP

Substitute fresh red bell pepper for the pimiento for a wonderful flavor and to boost the amount of vitamin C. Also, 1½ cups of cooked millet or cornmeal mush may be substituted for tofu.

Tofu Mayonnaise

Most mayonnaise is quite high in fat because of the high oil content. This one is not only egg-free, but oil-free as well. It's also quite tasty and great for salad recipes.

INGREDIENTS

⅓	cup	raw sunflower seeds *or* rinsed raw, cashews
⅓	cup	water
12.3 ounces		firm, silken tofu
2½	tbsp	lemon juice
¾	tsp	salt
½	tsp	garlic powder
1	tsp	onion powder

STEPS

1. Combine all ingredients in a blender and blend until smooth. A spatula may be used to stir during the blending process, but carefully!
2. Chill to thicken.
3. Keeps for 7-10 days in refrigerator.

MAKES 1¼ CUPS

PER 2 TABLESPOONS	
CALORIES	45
PROTEIN	4 g
CARBOHYDRATES	1.5 g
FIBER	1 g
FAT	3 g
SODIUM	100 mg

Seven-Layer Mexican Dip

A perfect dish to make for a festive gathering

INGREDIENTS

2	cups *or* 2 cans	pinto beans, drained
½	cup	diced tomatoes, drained
2	tsp	**"No Alarm" Chili Powder,** *page 41*
1	clove	pressed garlic
½	tsp	dried oregano
1	recipe	**Guacamole,** *page 64*
12.3 ounces		firm, silken tofu
2	tbsp	lemon juice
½	tsp	salt
½	tsp	onion powder
2	medium	vine-ripened tomatoes, diced
3		green onions, thinly sliced
½	cup	black olives, sliced

STEPS

1. Blend pinto beans and diced tomatoes, chili powder, garlic, and oregano in a blender until chunky.
2. Spread into 9" x 13" casserole dish.
3. Prepare **Guacamole** according to recipe. Spread over bean mixture.
4. Blend tofu, lemon juice, salt, and onion powder in the blender until smooth. Spread tofu mixture over guacamole.
5. Top with diced tomatoes, sliced onions, and sliced black olives.
6. Chill for at least 1 hour. Serve with tortilla chips.

MAKES 15 SERVINGS

PER ½ CUP	
CALORIES	115
PROTEIN	6 g
CARBOHYDRATES	10 g
FIBER	4 g
FAT	6.5 g
SODIUM	360 mg

Guacamole

No fiesta is complete without guacamole!

INGREDIENTS

2		ripe avocados (about 2 cups)
1	tbsp	chopped onion, or to taste
¼	tsp	garlic powder *or*
1	small	garlic clove, pressed
1	tbsp	lemon juice
½	tsp	salt
⅓	cup	finely diced tomato

STEPS

1 Mash avocados with a fork, or whiz in a small food processor.

2 Add remaining ingredients and stir to mix.

MAKES 2½ CUPS

PER ¼ CUP	
CALORIES	75
PROTEIN	1 g
CARBOHYDRATES	4.5 g
FIBER	3 g
FAT	6 g
SODIUM	120 mg

COOK'S TIP

If not serving the guacamole immediately, cover with 1 teaspoon lemon juice to maintain green color. Pour off lemon juice and stir before serving.

Fresh Avocado Salsa

Garden fresh cherry tomatoes and just-pulled corn makes this salsa absolutely magnificent.

INGREDIENTS

2		avocados, diced
2	ears	raw corn, cut off cob
1	pint	grape *or* cherry tomatoes, quartered
1	can	black beans
		juice of 1-2 limes, to taste
3	tbsp	fresh cilantro, chopped
¼	tsp	salt *or* to taste

STEPS

1 Pour black beans into colander and rinse.

2 Combine all ingredients in medium bowl and toss mix.

3 Serve with tortilla chips. Baked! Tostitos Scoops! are ideal to serve with this salsa.

MAKES 6 CUPS

PER ½ CUP	
CALORIES	90
PROTEIN	3.5 g
CARBOHYDRATES	14 g
FIBER	4.5 g
FAT	4 g
SODIUM	160 mg

Hot Broccoli Dip

Especially around the holidays, this dip is very well received. It can be made ahead and reheated, adding the toasted almonds just before it goes on the table.

INGREDIENTS

4	cups	fresh chopped broccoli *or* 10-oz. package frozen chopped broccoli
1	medium	onion, chopped
4-oz can		sliced *or* chopped mushrooms, drained
1–2	cloves	garlic, freshly pressed
½	cup	sliced toasted almonds

SAUCE INGREDIENTS:

1⅓	cups	water
¼	cup	raw, rinsed cashews
1½	tbsp	tahini
2	tsp	lemon juice
1	tsp	salt
2	tbsp	nutritional yeast flakes
1½	tsp	onion powder
½	tsp	garlic powder
1	tbsp	cornstarch

STEPS

1. Cook the broccoli while the sauce is being prepared. If using fresh, steam the broccoli with the chopped onion using a small steamer or in a small amount of water.

2. If using frozen broccoli, it may be cooked in the box in the microwave for 6 minutes, or follow directions on the box for stove-top preparation. Press any liquid out of the broccoli.

TO MAKE THE SAUCE:

1. Blend the sauce ingredients in blender until smooth. Heat in large saucepan over medium-high heat until thickened.

2. Add broccoli, onion, mushrooms, and garlic and heat just until bubbly.

3. Add toasted almonds just before serving so they remain crisp.

4. Serve hot with dipping corn chips.

MAKES 12 SERVINGS

PER ⅓ CUP	
CALORIES	120
PROTEIN	5 g
CARBOHYDRATES	10 g
FIBER	4.5 g
FAT	8 g
SODIUM	205 mg

Onion Dill Dip

The perfect addition to any party or picnic menu. Again, they won't believe it's tofu!

INGREDIENTS

1	recipe	**Tofu Mayonnaise,** *page 63*
1	tbsp	lemon juice
1¼	tsp	dill weed
1½	tsp	onion powder
		salt to taste

STEPS

1. Combine all ingredients in a bowl and stir to mix.

2. Serve with chips (Baked Lays, baked tortilla chips) or raw veggies.

MAKES 2¼ CUPS

PER 2 TABLESPOONS	
CALORIES	45
PROTEIN	4 g
CARBOHYDRATES	2 g
FIBER	1 g
FAT	3 g
SODIUM	100 mg

Spinach Salad

Bags of prewashed spinach make this salad convenient to make, and it's a welcomed change from conventional tossed salad.

INGREDIENTS

½	cup	slivered almonds
2	quarts	fresh spinach
¼	cup	grated carrots
¼	cup	lemon juice
½	tsp	dried basil leaves
⅛	tsp	thyme
2	tbsp	sesame seeds
⅛	tsp	onion salt
2	cloves	garlic, pressed

STEPS

1 Toast almonds at 300°F for 10 minutes or until lightly toasted. Watch almonds closely to prevent burning. Set aside.

2 Carefully wash and tear spinach into bite-sized pieces. Add carrots.

3 Combine remaining ingredients and shake in a jar to make a dressing.

4 Toss spinach, carrots, and almonds with dressing just before serving.

MAKES 6 SERVINGS

PER SERVING	
CALORIES	150
PROTEIN	6 g
CARBOHYDRATES	9 g
FIBER	4 g
FAT	12 g
SODIUM	65 mg

Apple Walnut Salad for Two

Commonly known as Waldorf salad, this original recipe was created not by the chef, but by the maître d'hôtel of New York's Waldorf-Astoria in 1896.

INGREDIENTS

½	cup	Vegenaise
1	tsp	honey
1	large	apple (Braeburn, Red, *or* Golden Delicious)
2	tbsp	walnuts, coarsely chopped
1½	tbsp	raisins

STEPS

1 Combine Vegenaise and honey in a mixing bowl. (**Tofu Mayonnaise,** *page 63*, may also be used, but the higher fat version works better.)

2 Core and dice apple and add to mayonnaise mixture along with walnuts and raisins.

3 Mix well and chill before serving.

MAKES 2 SERVINGS

PER ½ RECIPE	
CALORIES	210
PROTEIN	6.5 g
CARBOHYDRATES	28.5 g
FIBER	4 g
FAT	10 g
SODIUM	225 mg

HEALTH TIP

A medium-size apple contains about 80 calories and is a good source of potassium and fiber. The fiber in apples is a mix of soluble and insoluble fiber, providing heart health and colon cancer prevention benefits at the same time.

Beets & Baby Greens Salad

After you've tasted fresh beets, you will never go back to eating canned or bottled beets. And after trying them raw, you may never bother to cook them again!

INGREDIENTS

1	medium	fresh beet
4	cups	baby salad greens
¼	cup	chopped onion of your choice, sliced
½	cup	coarsely chopped walnuts

PER 1½ CUP	
CALORIES	125
PROTEIN	4 g
CARBOHYDRATES	8 g
FIBER	3 g
FAT	9.5 g
SODIUM	30 mg

STEPS

1. Peel and grate beet on coarse side of grater.

2. Toss greens, onions, and cucumber together and create a bed of greens on salad plates. Top with grated beets and walnuts.

3. Serve with **Ruby Raspberry Dressing,** *page 67.*

   MAKES 4 SERVINGS

Ruby Raspberry Dressing

Beautiful and full of flavor, this dressing packs a great nutritional punch.

INGREDIENTS

½	cup	white grape raspberry juice concentrate
½	cup	lemon juice
¼	cup	flaxseed oil
¼	cup	olive oil
1	tsp	Vegesal *or* salt
2	tsp	Instant Clear Jel

PER 2 TABLESPOONS	
CALORIES	95
PROTEIN	.1 g
CARBOHYDRATES	5.5 g
FIBER	.1 g
FAT	8.5 g
SODIUM	390 mg

STEPS

1. Place all ingredients except the Instant Clear Jel in a blender.

2. Blend well and sprinkle Instant Clear Jel into dressing while blender is running on medium speed.

3. Chill and serve over any fresh, tossed salad.

   MAKES 1½ CUPS

"I have often wondered why people take better care of their cars than their bodies. I have yet to meet a person who said, 'God has a plan as to when my car should die, and I do not need to worry about it.'" — NEIL NEDLEY, M.D.

Dill Dressing

Fresh onion, garlic, and lemon juice give this dressing a real punch. Fresh dill makes it even better.

INGREDIENTS

1	cup	raw cashews, rinsed
1	cup	water
⅓	cup	lemon juice
¾	tsp	salt
1½	tsp	onion powder *or*
1½	tbsp	fresh onion
½	tsp	garlic powder *or*
1	clove	garlic
½	tsp	dried dill weed *or*
1	tbsp	fresh dill

STEPS

1 Blend all ingredients until smooth.

2 Chill and serve.

MAKES 2¼ CUPS

PER 2 TABLESPOONS	
CALORIES	75
PROTEIN	2.5 g
CARBOHYDRATES	4 g
FIBER	.5 g
FAT	6 g
SODIUM	100 mg

Toasted Sesame Dressing

Any salad steps up a notch when tossed with this tart but savory dressing.

INGREDIENTS

¼	cup	raw cashews, rinsed
⅓	cup	nutritional yeast flakes
⅓	cup	lemon juice
½	cup	water
½	cup	toasted sesame oil
½	cup	olive oil
1	tsp	onion powder
1	tsp	ground marjoram
2	tsp	salt
2½	tbsp	honey
2	cloves	fresh garlic

STEPS

1 Blend all ingredients in blender until smooth. Keeps in refrigerator for about 2 weeks.

MAKES 2 CUPS

PER 2 TABLESPOONS	
CALORIES	125
PROTEIN	1.5 g
CARBOHYDRATES	5 g
FIBER	1 g
FAT	11.5 g
SODIUM	260 mg

COOK'S TIP

This dressing is excellent drizzled inside a tortilla wrap filled with hummus, sliced tomatoes, cucumbers, lettuce, and olives.

Italian Dressing

This zesty and versatile dressing keeps in the refrigerator for 10 to 14 days.

INGREDIENTS

¼	cup	lemon juice
¼	cup	olive oil
½	cup	water
1	tbsp	honey
2	tsp	chicken-style seasoning
½	tsp	salt
1	large	clove garlic
½	tsp	Italian seasonings
1	tsp	parsley
2	tsp	Instant Clear Jel

STEPS

1. Blend all ingredients except Instant Clear Jel in blender until smooth.
2. Sprinkle in Instant Clear Jel while blending.
3. This dressing will thicken further as it chills.

MAKES 1⅓ CUPS

PER 2 TABLESPOONS	
CALORIES	55
PROTEIN	.1 g
CARBOHYDRATES	2.5 g
FIBER	0 g
FAT	5 g
SODIUM	205 mg

Ranch Dressing

Fresh lemon juice is best when it comes to salad dressings—especially this one.

INGREDIENTS

¼	cup	raw sunflower seeds
¼	cup	tahini
3	tbsp	fresh onion in chunks
¾	tsp	salt
¾	cup	water
4	tbsp	lemon juice
1	large	clove garlic
½	tsp	dill weed
2	tsp	parsley flakes

STEPS

1. Combine all ingredients except dill weed and parsley flakes in a blender and blend until smooth.
2. Add herbs and blend again for about 5 seconds.

MAKES 1⅔ CUPS

PER 2 TABLESPOONS	
CALORIES	35
PROTEIN	1 g
CARBOHYDRATES	2 g
FIBER	.5 g
FAT	3 g
SODIUM	140 mg

Southwestern Salad

Many restaurants serve a similar salad and include chunks of chicken breast. Soy Curls prepared with chicken-style seasoning will add taste and texture to this salad, though it's quite good as is.

INGREDIENTS

6	cups	romaine lettuce, torn
1		avocado, diced
16-oz. can		black beans, drained
1	cup	corn, canned, fresh, or frozen
2	cups	diced tomatoes, canned *or* fresh
1		cucumber, diced
½	cup	red onion, chopped
1	recipe	**Mexi-Texi Ranch Dressing**
½	cup	fresh cilantro, chopped

STEPS

1 Place 1½ cups of the lettuce on individual plates. Top each salad with ⅓ cup **Mexi-Texi Ranch Dressing** (see recipe below).

2 Layer with black beans, avocado, corn, tomatoes, cucumber, and red onion. Sprinkle each salad with 2 tablespoons of cilantro.

3 Serve with corn chips.

MAKES 4 LARGE SALADS

MEXI-TEXI RANCH DRESSING

Combine 1 cup **Salsa**, *page 62*, and 1 cup **Ranch Dressing**, *page 69*, in a bowl and mix well.

MAKES 2 CUPS

PER SALAD	
CALORIES	375
PROTEIN	16.5 g
CARBOHYDRATES	56 g
FIBER	19.6 g
FAT	13 g
SODIUM	625 mg

Dilled Cucumbers

> **COOK'S TIP**
> If in a hurry, place several ice cubes on the cucumbers to chill.

Summer's bounty from the garden usually includes lots of cucumbers, and this is a refreshing way to serve them. Sliced sweet onion or chopped spring onion tops may be added as well.

INGREDIENTS

1	large	cucumber
3	tbsp	lemon juice
¼	tsp	salt
1	tsp	dill weed
¼	cup	water

STEPS

1 Peel cucumber in a striped fashion and slice into rounds.

2 Toss with remaining ingredients. Salt to taste. Much of the salt will remain in the lemon water.

3 Chill and serve.

MAKES 6 SERVINGS

PER ⅙ RECIPE	
CALORIES	10
PROTEIN	.5 g
CARBOHYDRATES	2.5 g
FIBER	.5 g
FAT	0 g
SODIUM	60 mg

"Daniel's clearness of mind and firmness of purpose, his strength of intellect in acquiring knowledge, were due in a great degree to the plainness of his diet, in connection with his life of prayer." — ELLEN G. WHITE

Tomato Basil Salad

The time to make this salad is when the tomatoes come in fresh from the garden. I like to peel the tomatoes so they are perfectly tender. Outstanding with **Gazpacho**, *page 74*, and **Honey Wheat Bread**, *page 54*, with avocado slices on a warm summer day.

INGREDIENTS

3		vine-ripened tomatoes
½	small	red onion, thinly sliced
15-oz can		white beans, drained
¼	cup	fresh basil leaves, chopped
3	tbsp	lemon juice
1	tbsp	olive oil
½	tsp	salt

STEPS

1. Slice tomatoes into ½-inch wedges, cutting again if tomatoes are large. Place into a medium-size bowl.

2. Combine with onion and beans that have been drained and rinsed.

3. Add basil, lemon juice, olive oil, and salt and toss to mix. Chill slightly and allow flavors to blend.

MAKES 4 SERVINGS

PER 1 CUP	
CALORIES	165
PROTEIN	9 g
CARBOHYDRATES	28.5 g
FIBER	6.5 g
FAT	3 g
SODIUM	300 mg

COOK'S TIP

If fresh basil is not available, use 1½ teaspoons of dried basil. It is still delicious!

Tofu Egg Salad

Superior in taste and nutrition, this vegan version is easier to prepare than a conventional egg salad. Perfect in a pita and a nice tea sandwich filling.

INGREDIENTS

14	ounces	fresh, firm tofu
½	cup	finely chopped celery
¾	cup	Vegenaise *or* **Tofu Mayonnaise,** *page 63*
¼	cup	sweet lemon pickle relish
¾	tsp	turmeric
1	tsp	onion powder
½	tsp	garlic powder
2	tsp	chicken-style seasoning
		salt to taste

STEPS

1. Mash tofu until fine in medium bowl.

2. Add remaining ingredients and mix well.

MAKES 4 SERVINGS

PER ½ CUP	
CALORIES	90
PROTEIN	6 g
CARBOHYDRATES	8.5 g
FIBER	1.5 g
FAT	4 g
SODIUM	100 mg

Greek Salad

Another garden-to-table recipe, this salad is delicious with or without the tofu.

INGREDIENTS

½	pound	tofu, extra firm
2	tbsp	chicken-style seasoning
2	cups	water
2½	cups	tomatoes, diced
3	cups	cucumbers, peeled and diced
½	cup	red onion, chopped
½	tsp	garlic powder *or* 1 clove, pressed
¼	cup	lemon juice
2	tbsp	olive oil (optional)
1	tsp	salt
½	tsp	oregano leaves
¼	cup	fresh basil, chopped (or 2 tsp dried)
1	cup	pitted whole black olives

STEPS

1. Dice tofu into ¾-inch cubes. Boil tofu for 15 minutes in the 2 cups water with the chicken-style seasoning added. Drain and cool.

2. Combine with remaining ingredients and toss.

3. Chill and allow flavors to blend.

MAKES 8 SERVINGS

PER ½ CUP SERVING, WITHOUT OLIVE OIL	
CALORIES	60
PROTEIN	3.5 g
CARBOHYDRATES	5.5 g
FIBER	1.5 g
FAT	3 g
SODIUM	540 mg

Kale Salad

Colorful and calcium-rich, this salad keeps well in the refrigerator for several days, and the raw kale is surprisingly tender.

INGREDIENTS

⅓	cup	fresh lemon juice
3	tbsp	Bragg Liquid Aminos
⅓	cup	water
½ 1	tsp	garlic powder *or* large clove, pressed
1	tsp	onion powder
7	cups	fresh, raw kale, finely chopped
4		scallions, chopped
½	cup	black olives, sliced
⅓	cup	raw sunflower seeds
½	cup	red bell pepper, diced

STEPS

1. Combine first five ingredients in a jar and shake to make the dressing.

2. Toss kale, olives, and scallions in a large bowl. Pour the dressing over the salad and stir to mix. Allow to marinate about an hour or overnight.

3. Just before serving, add the sunflower seeds and red bell pepper.

MAKES 8 CUPS

PER 1 CUP	
CALORIES	150
PROTEIN	6.5 g
CARBOHYDRATES	12 g
FIBER	4 g
FAT	10.5 g
SODIUM	480 mg

Fruit Salad

If you are trying to lower your sodium intake, eat more fruit. And to keep it interesting, make some creative fruit salads. Around the holiday season, a beautiful and festive combination is fresh pineapple, apples, grapes, star fruit, and pomegranate seeds. They look like jewels!

INGREDIENTS

20-oz can		pineapple chunks *or* tidbits in juice
1	large	apple, cored and diced
1		banana, sliced
1	cup	sliced strawberries *or* blueberries

STEPS

1. Mix and serve. Other fruits of your choice (cherries, kiwi, grapes, orange sections, pears, peaches, and melons in season).

2. If served early in the day, chopped nuts, coconut, raisins, dates, or other chopped dried fruit can be added.

MAKES 5 SERVINGS

PER 1 CUP	
CALORIES	110
PROTEIN	1 g
CARBOHYDRATES	28.5 g
FIBER	3.5 g
FAT	.3 g
SODIUM	2 mg

Ultimate Gazpacho

Gazpacho is a traditional Spanish soup, served cold, that you can make as chunky as you like. Raw and robust, the flavor and nutrition are absolutely bursting out of this soup.

INGREDIENTS

4	cups	tomatoes
1	cup	cucumber
2	tbsp	olive oil
⅓	cup	lemon juice
½	tsp	salt
1	medium	garlic clove
½	cup	red bell pepper, finely diced
¼	cup	onion, chopped
½	cup	cilantro *or* parsley, chopped

STEPS

1 Pulse in a blender 2 cups of the tomatoes and the cup of cucumber, olive oil, lemon juice, salt, and garlic. Pour into a large bowl. This mixture should be thick and slightly chunky.

2 All the remaining vegetables, including the remaining tomatoes, should be chopped or diced very fine.

3 Mix the chopped vegetables with the ingredients that have been blended.

4 Serve cold on a hot summer day, or any time!

MAKES 6 SERVINGS

PER 1¼ CUP	
CALORIES	70
PROTEIN	2 g
CARBOHYDRATES	10 g
FIBER	2 g
FAT	3.5 g
SODIUM	205 mg

French Onion Soup

Again we thank the French for another classic recipe. Minus the cheese, this version is still delicious and somewhat lower in sodium. Perfect for supper fare on a chilly evening.

INGREDIENTS

3	medium	onions, thinly sliced
1	tbsp	olive oil
8	cups	water
3	tbsp	chicken-style seasoning
½	cup	Bragg Liquid Aminos
2	tbsp	onion powder
1	tbsp	maple syrup

STEPS

1 Sauté onions in a large pot in the olive oil until slightly browned.

2 Add water and seasonings and allow to simmer for 20 minutes.

3 For a real treat, top each cup of soup with a few croutons, then top with a slice of soy cheese. Place the bowl in the microwave on high for about 30 seconds to melt the cheese.

MAKES 8 SERVINGS

PER 1¼ CUP	
CALORIES	45
PROTEIN	2.5 g
CARBOHYDRATES	9 g
FIBER	1 g
FAT	1 g
SODIUM	850 mg

Soy Curls Noodle Soup

This vegan version works just as well as the often-prescribed chicken noodle soup for those feeling a little under the weather—in fact, it's probably better!

COOK'S TIP

A nice addition to this soup is a handful of thoroughly washed fresh spinach. Add it to the soup and continue cooking another 3 minutes. If Soy Curls are unavailable, cooked garbanzos can be used.

INGREDIENTS

1	tbsp	minced garlic
½	cup	chopped onion
6	cups	water
2	cups	dry whole-grain pasta, ribbon style if available
1	cup	Soy Curls
1½	tbsp	chicken-style seasoning
1	tsp	dried parsley *or*
2	tbsp	fresh parsley, finely chopped

STEPS

1. In a large pot, lightly steam onion and garlic in ½ cup of the water.

2. Place remaining water, pasta, and chicken-style seasonings into a pot and bring it to a boil. Add remaining ingredients and bring to a boil. Allow to boil gently for 8 to 10 minutes.

3. Cook on medium heat until pasta is tender. Add Soy Curls and parsley.

MAKES 6 SERVINGS

PER 1 CUP	
CALORIES	300
PROTEIN	13.5 g
CARBOHYDRATES	20 g
FIBER	1 g
FAT	2 g
SODIUM	150 mg

Broccoli Soup

Tahini and nutritional yeast flakes provide a cheesy flavor without any dairy products in this flavorful cream soup. Try cauliflower, asparagus, or celery instead of broccoli.

INGREDIENTS

5½	cups	unsweetened soymilk *or* nut milk
3	cups	fresh broccoli, chopped
2	tbsp	nutritional yeast flakes
½	tsp	garlic powder or
1	clove	pressed
½	cup	chopped, steamed onions *or*
2	tbsp	dry onion flakes
1	tsp	salt
1	tbsp	tahini
¼	cup	cornstarch
¼	tsp	turmeric

STEPS

1. Heat 4 cups milk, nutritional yeast flakes, garlic powder, tahini, and salt in a medium saucepan, but do not boil.

2. Place broccoli and onions in steamer and steam until tender.

3. Mix cornstarch with remaining 1½ cups milk. Add to heated milk and cook on low heat, stirring constantly until thickened.

4. Add steamed broccoli and onion to thickened soup. Serve hot.

MAKES 8 SERVINGS

PER 1 CUP	
CALORIES	130
PROTEIN	8.5 g
CARBOHYDRATES	16.5 g
FIBER	3.2 g
FAT	4.5 g
SODIUM	320 mg

HEALTH TIP

Another excellent source of potassium, one cup of broccoli contains 460 milligrams.

Butternut Squash Soup

Rich in beta-carotene, potassium, and other minerals, butternut squash is one of the most delicious winter squashes. They are easy to grow, so be sure to plant some in your garden and look forward to serving this satisfying soup on a chilly winter day.

INGREDIENTS

1	medium	butternut squash
2	medium	apples
1	medium	onion
4	cups	water
1	tsp	salt
13.5-oz can		coconut milk
		dash of cayenne (optional)

STEPS

1 Peel butternut squash and cut into large chunks. You will need about 6 cups. Cut apples and onion into large chunks.

2 Combine the squash, apples, and onion in a large pot with the water. Cook until tender.

3 Puree cooked ingredients in blender. Pour back into pot. Add salt, coconut milk, and cayenne if desired and stir until blended.

4 Bring to a boil and serve hot.

MAKES 8 CUPS

PER 1 CUP	
CALORIES	155
PROTEIN	2 g
CARBOHYDRATES	19 g
FIBER	3 g
FAT	9 g
SODIUM	300 mg

Cuban Black Bean Soup

Soup and salad with a whole grain bread make a complete meal when you serve a hearty bean soup like this one.

INGREDIENTS

1	pound	dry black beans
7	cups	water
1		onion, chopped
2	cloves	fresh garlic, pressed
2	stalks	celery
1	tsp	olive oil or
2	tbsp	water
½	tsp	dried oregano
1	tsp	cumin (optional)
15-oz can		stewed tomatoes
1	tsp	salt

STEPS

1 Sort and rinse black beans and cook with water overnight on low in a crockpot. Remove liquid to achieve desired consistency.

2 In a skillet, sauté in oil or steam onion, garlic, and celery until soft. Add oregano and cumin if desired.

3 Add the sautéed mixture, salt, and the tomatoes to the crockpot. Continue to cook for 30 minutes or less.

MAKES 8 SERVINGS

PER 1¼ CUP	
CALORIES	215
PROTEIN	12.5 g
CARBOHYDRATES	39 g
FIBER	9 g
FAT	1.5 g
SODIUM	400 mg

Cajun Gumbo des Herbes

"Des herbes" means vegetable gumbo. Even the "chicken" in this version is a vegetable!

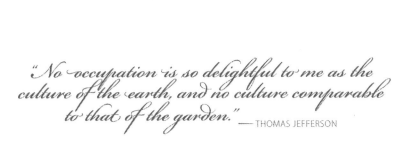

INGREDIENTS

2	tbsp	olive oil
2	tbsp	flour
6	cups	water
1	tbsp	chicken-style seasoning
1	cup	dry Soy Curls *or*
2	cups	seasoned tofu
1	bunch	scallions, with tops
¾	cup	fresh parsley, chopped fine
½	cup	green pepper, diced
15-oz can		diced tomatoes
2		bay leaves
1	dash	cayenne
½	tsp	salt, *or* to taste
1	cup	fresh *or* frozen okra, sliced
2	cups	cooked brown rice

STEPS

1. Combine olive oil and flour to make a roux in a heavy-bottom soup pot. Brown this mixture on medium-high heat, stirring constantly, until the color of peanut butter.

2. Stir in water and bouillon and bring to a boil.

3. Add remaining ingredients, except okra and rice, and allow to return to a boil. Simmer on low about 15 minutes

4. Add okra and cook an additional 10 minutes.

5. Serve in bowls with a scoop of brown rice.

MAKES 8 CUPS

PER 1 CUP	
CALORIES	160
PROTEIN	8 g
CARBOHYDRATES	18 g
FIBER	2.5 g
FAT	7 g
SODIUM	750 mg

"No occupation is so delightful to me as the culture of the earth, and no culture comparable to that of the garden." — THOMAS JEFFERSON

Lentil Tomato Stew

We can thank Charlotte and Katrina (aka "Charlie" and "Bean") for this tasty stew that's quick and hearty.

INGREDIENTS

1	cup	dry lentils
3	cups	water
1	can	diced tomatoes
1	medium	onion, diced
3	cloves	garlic, sliced
1	tsp	dried basil
½	cup	quick-cooking brown rice
½	tsp	salt, *or* to taste

STEPS

1. Bring lentils and water to a boil in a large saucepan. Turn to low heat and simmer for 30 minutes.
2. Add remaining ingredients and simmer an additional 15 to 20 minutes.
3. Add water if more "soup" is desired.

MAKES 4 SERVINGS

PER 1¼ CUP	
CALORIES	270
PROTEIN	16 g
CARBOHYDRATES	51 g
FIBER	16.5 g
FAT	1 g
SODIUM	360 mg

"Trust in the Lord, and do good; so shalt thou dwell in the land, and verily thou shalt be fed." — PSALM 37:3

Ratatouille

Harvest time is the perfect time to prepare this vegetable stew. Add some black beans, and you have a complete entrée.

INGREDIENTS

1	large	onion, chopped
1		green pepper, diced
1	clove	fresh garlic, pressed
2	medium	zucchini, diced
1	medium	eggplant, diced
3		tomatoes, diced
1	tbsp	olive oil
½	cup	water
1	tsp	salt
½	tsp	dried basil
¼	tsp	dried oregano

STEPS

1. Use a large, heavy-bottomed saucepan with a lid. Sauté the onion, garlic, and green pepper in olive oil while dicing the other vegetables.
2. Add zucchini, eggplant, and water and stir. Cover and steam for 5 minutes. Add tomatoes, cover, and simmer for 30 minutes or until all vegetables are well cooked.
3. Uncover and turn up the heat to allow some of the liquid to evaporate. Serve over cooked brown rice.

MAKES 8 SERVINGS

PER 1¼ CUP	
CALORIES	60
PROTEIN	2.5 g
CARBOHYDRATES	12 g
FIBER	4.5 g
FAT	1.5 g
SODIUM	305 mg

Red Lentil Soup

India's protein-rich classic dish has many varieties, and this one is simple and savory. Variations can include the addition of different squashes.

COOK'S TIP

See Special Ingredients, *page 41*, for **Mild Curry Powder** recipe.

INGREDIENTS

1	medium	onion, chopped
1		red bell pepper, diced
3		carrots, sliced
2	medium	potatoes, diced
1	cup	red lentils, rinsed
4	cups	water
1	tbsp	chicken-style seasoning
2	cloves	garlic, minced
1	tbsp	mild curry powder
½	tsp	salt, *or* to taste
2	tbsp	olive oil

STEPS

1. Steam onions and red pepper in a small amount of water in a heavy-bottom stock pot.
2. Add carrots, potatoes, lentils, and water. Bring to a boil, then cover and simmer for about an hour.
3. Add remaining ingredients and simmer a few minutes more.
4. Serve over brown rice or with whole-wheat chapatis or pita bread.

MAKES 8 SERVINGS

PER CUP	
CALORIES	175
PROTEIN	7.5 g
CARBOHYDRATES	27 g
FIBER	4.5 g
FAT	4 g
SODIUM	370 mg

Mom's Chili

This chili takes just 10 minutes to make, and it's good!

COOK'S TIP

See Special Ingredients on *page 41* for **"No Alarm" Chili Powder** recipe.

INGREDIENTS

1	cup	onion, chopped
1	cup	green pepper, diced
1	cup	vegeburger (optional)
26.5-oz can		non-chunky-style spaghetti sauce
16-oz can		dark red kidney beans
14.5-oz can		diced tomatoes with juice
½	tbsp	**"No Alarm" Chili Powder**, *page 41*
½	cup	water

STEPS

1. Steam onion and green pepper in small amount of water in a large saucepan.
2. Add remaining ingredients and bring to a boil. Turn down and simmer for a few minutes.
3. Serve over cooked brown rice, over a baked potato, or in a bowl with **Whole-Wheat Bread**, *page 55*, or crackers.

MAKES 6 SERVINGS

PER 1¼ CUP	
CALORIES	200
PROTEIN	12.5 g
CARBOHYDRATES	30.5 g
FIBER	10 g
FAT	4 g
SODIUM	900 mg

Vegetable Barley Soup

Quick and hearty!

INGREDIENTS

1	small	onion, chopped
1	clove	fresh garlic, pressed
1	stalk	celery, sliced
1	tbsp	olive oil *or*
2	tbsp	water
1		carrot, diced
1	medium	potato, diced
3	cups	water
2	tsp	chicken-style seasoning
14.5-oz can		whole tomatoes
¼	cup	dry barley
½	cup	garbanzo beans
1	tsp	dried basil
1	tsp	parsley flakes
1	cup	okra, sliced

STEPS

1. In a Dutch oven, steam or sauté onion, garlic, and celery until tender.

2. Add all remaining ingredients except okra. Bring to a boil, cover, and simmer for 10 minutes.

3. Add okra and continue cooking for 15 minutes, until okra is tender.

MAKES 6 SERVINGS

PER 1 CUP	
CALORIES	125
PROTEIN	3.5 g
CARBOHYDRATES	22 g
FIBER	4.5 g
FAT	3 g
SODIUM	300 mg

"Grains, fruits, nuts, and vegetables constitute the diet chosen for us by our Creator. They impart a strength, a power of endurance, and a vigor of intellect, that are not afforded by a more complex and stimulating diet." — ELLEN G. WHITE

Navy Bean Soup

For years I thought bean soup would lack flavor without what most people consider an essential ingredient: a ham bone. Yet herbs, vegetables, and salt in combination with these navy beans make an incredibly delicious soup, with no animal fat.

COOK'S TIP

Raw carrots, celery, and onions can be added to the crockpot in the morning; then continue cooking for several hours.

INGREDIENTS

1	pound	dry navy beans (2½ cups)
7	cups	water
1		bay leaf
1	cup	grated carrots
1	cup	chopped celery
1	cup	chopped onion
1	tsp	chicken-style seasoning
½	tsp	salt
1	tsp	onion powder
½	tsp	garlic powder
½	tsp	ground marjoram
¼	tsp	sage
¼	tsp	thyme

STEPS

1. Cook beans in a crockpot on low overnight with the water and bay leaf.
2. Steam carrots, celery, and onion until tender.
3. Combine steamed veggies with beans and add remaining ingredients.

MAKES 8 SERVINGS

PER 1 CUP	
CALORIES	195
PROTEIN	12 g
CARBOHYDRATES	35 g
FIBER	14 g
FAT	1 g
SODIUM	250 mg

Split Pea Soup

This high-fiber soup has almost no fat, yet it is flavorful and satisfying. Enjoy it any time of the year.

INGREDIENTS

2	cups	dry split peas
7½	cups	water
1	large	onion, chopped
1		bay leaf
1	large	carrot, sliced
2	stalks	celery, sliced
1	clove	garlic, pressed (optional)
2	tsp	salt

STEPS

1. Sort and wash split peas. Cook the peas, onion, and bay leaf with water in large sauce pan for about 45 minutes by bringing them to a boil on high, then reduce heat and cover.
2. Add remaining ingredients and simmer ½ hour more or until vegetables are tender.

MAKES 6 CUPS

PER ¾ CUP	
CALORIES	170
PROTEIN	11.5 g
CARBOHYDRATES	32 g
FIBER	6.5 g
FAT	0.5 g
SODIUM	600 mg

"Research makes evident that foods high in fiber lead to a lower rise in blood sugar, and as a result, require less insulin to handle the meal."
— NEIL NEDLEY, M.D.

Linguine With Artichoke Hearts

Sal's Bistro prepares a pasta entrée very similar to this one and provided the idea for this recipe.

INGREDIENTS

8	ounces	dry linguine
2	tbsp	olive oil
1	small	onion, chopped
1	clove	fresh garlic, pressed
3	large	mushrooms
13.75-oz can		artichoke hearts
½	cup	**Spaghetti Sauce,** *page 99*
½	tsp	dried basil
½	tsp	salt
1	medium	vine-ripe tomato

STEPS

1. Bring 3 quarts of water to a boil. Cook linguine according to directions.

2. Sauté onion and garlic in ½ tablespoon of the olive oil for 3 minutes in a large skillet. Add mushrooms that have been stemmed and quartered into wedges and continue sautéing for 5 minutes.

3. Drain artichoke hearts and chop in half each way. Add artichokes, sauce, basil, and salt to the skillet. Stir, and continue to cook on low heat.

4. Dip tomato into the boiling water with the linguine for 15 seconds. Rinse with cold water and remove the skin. Slice into very thin wedges and add to the skillet. Cook only several minutes longer.

5. Drain the linguine when al dente (done "to the bite") and add to the skillet. Add the remaining 1½ tablespoons olive oil and toss.

MAKES 4 SERVINGS

PER SERVING	
CALORIES	205
PROTEIN	7.5 g
CARBOHYDRATES	31 g
FIBER	9.5 g
FAT	8 g
SODIUM	600 mg

Spinach Ricotta-style Filling

Lasagna, manicotti, and stuffed pasta shells are all scrumptious with this delicious tofu filling. Easy to prepare and rich in tryptophan and B vitamins, these Italian favorites are great make-ahead entrées.

INGREDIENTS

14	ounces	tofu, extra firm, mashed
1½	cups	sautéed, chopped onion
10	ounces	frozen chopped spinach
2	tsp	garlic powder
2	tsp	sweet basil
1	tsp	salt
1	tbsp	honey
1	tbsp	lemon juice
2	tbsp	nutritional yeast flakes
½	tsp	oregano

STEPS

1. Cook spinach, using directions on box or by placing the whole box in the microwave for 6 minutes.

2. Combine spinach with remaining ingredients in large bowl and mix well.

3. Use for **Lasagna,** *page 83*, or for **Stuffed Shells** (see below).

MAKES 8 SERVINGS

PER ½ CUP	
CALORIES	105
PROTEIN	10.5 g
CARBOHYDRATES	9 g
FIBER	3.5 g
FAT	4.5 g
SODIUM	325 mg

COOK'S TIP

For **Stuffed Shells,** cook shells and fill with filling. Place in a casserole dish with the bottom covered with sauce. Spoon sauce across each shell but do not completely cover. Cover with foil, being careful not to touch shells. Bake 30 minutes at 350°F.

Lasagna

Perfect for a potluck, as it can be made ahead of time and serves a crowd.

INGREDIENTS

7	cups	**Spaghetti Sauce,** *page 99*
1	recipe	**Spinach Ricotta-style Filling,** *page 82*
½	pound	uncooked lasagna noodles
¾	cup	soy cheese or **Quick & Easy Cheese,** *page 62*
½	cup	water

PER 2 X 2-INCH SERVING	
CALORIES	154
PROTEIN	10.5 g
CARBOHYDRATES	19 g
FIBER	5 g
FAT	6 g
SODIUM	710 mg

Variation: Add steamed spinach, carrots, and/ or squash after layer of **Spinach Ricotta-style Filling.**

STEPS

1. Make layers in a 9" x 13" pan, starting with a layer of **Spaghetti Sauce,** then a layer of uncooked noodles, then a full recipe of **Spinach Ricotta-style Filling.** Top with another layer of noodles, and sprinkle the remaining sauce and the ½ cup water evenly over the top.

2. Cover and refrigerate overnight.

3. Soy cheese or **Quick & Easy Cheese** can be added just prior to baking, or if serving later, top with cheese prior to reheating. For best results, bake, allow to cool and set, and reheat prior to serving.

4. Bake at 350°F for 45 minutes.

MAKES 12 SERVINGS

COOK'S TIP

Another interesting way to prepare vegetarian lasagna is to slice zucchini lengthwise into ¼-inch flat strips for use in place of the lasagna noodles. Place the zucchini slices on an oil-sprayed baking sheet and add a sprinkle of salt and Italian seasonings. Bake at 425°F for 20 minutes, turning over once halfway through baking. Proceed with lasagna recipe.

Soy Curls Cacciatore

Soy Curls provide optimum nutrition, as well as taste and texture and incredible versatility. This is just one more traditional chicken recipe that works exceptionally well with Soy Curls. Presents well with brown rice or pasta.

INGREDIENTS

1½	cups	water with ½ tsp salt
1	cup	Soy Curls
1	cup	onion, diced
2	stalks	celery, diced
2	tsp	olive oil (optional)
28-oz can		diced tomatoes
2	tsp	chicken-style seasoning
1	clove	garlic, pressed

PER 1 CUP	
CALORIES	130
PROTEIN	5.5 g
CARBOHYDRATES	20 g
FIBER	4.7 g
FAT	4 g
SODIUM	940 mg

STEPS

1. Rehydrate Soy Curls in the salt water for 30 minutes.

2. In a nonstick skillet, sauté onion, garlic, and celery in olive oil or steam in small amount of water until tender.

3. Pour water off Soy Curls and add them to the mixture.

4. Add tomatoes and chicken-style seasoning* and simmer for 5 minutes.

5. Serve over cooked brown rice.

If chicken-style seasoning is not available, simply add ¼ teaspoon garlic powder, 1½ teaspoons onion powder, and ¼–½ teaspoon Italian seasonings.

MAKES 4 SERVINGS

"Daniel purposed in his heart that he would not defile himself with . . . the king's delicacies, nor with the wine which he drank." — DANIEL 1:8, NKJV

Veggie Patch Flatbread

As colorful and appealing as it is delicious, this casual fare is always very well received.

INGREDIENTS

2	12-inch	whole-wheat flatbread *or* pita bread loaves
1	tbsp	olive oil *or* water
1	medium	zucchini
1	medium	onion
2	cloves	fresh garlic, sliced
½		red *or* green bell pepper
¼	tsp	salt
3.5-oz can		sliced ripe olives
½	tsp	Italian seasoning
2	small	tomatoes
1	recipe	**Quick & Easy Cheese,** *page 62*

STEPS

1. Sauté or steam zucchini, onions, and pepper in oil or water for 5 minutes

2. Spread flatbread with **Quick & Easy Cheese** from which the pimiento has been omitted.

3. Arrange sliced tomatoes and sautéed vegetables on top of cheese, top with sliced olives, and sprinkle with Italian seasoning.

4. Bake at 350°F for 15 minutes using a pizza pan.

MAKES 8 SLICES

PER SLICE	
CALORIES	180
PROTEIN	8.5 g
CARBOHYDRATES	25 g
FIBER	4.5 g
FAT	7 g
SODIUM	670 mg

"Worship the Lord your God, and his blessing will be on your food and water. I will take away sickness from among you . . . I will give you a full life span." —EXODUS 23:25, 26, NIV

Shish Kabobs

This cooking method and presentation give a superb taste and appeal to simple food. Great make-ahead summer fare.

INGREDIENTS

1		red or green bell pepper
1	small	onion
12		cherry tomatoes
14	ounces	fresh, extra-firm tofu
1	recipe	**Italian Marinade,** *page 103*

STEPS

1. Dice tofu into 1-inch pieces. Slice pepper, zucchini, and onion into 1-inch pieces.

2. Place the tofu and all the vegetables in a bowl with the marinade and allow them to marinate for 30 minutes.

3. Make the shish kabobs, alternating the veggies and tofu. Place on a preheated grill or under the broiler for approximately 8 minutes. Rotate skewers and cook the other side for 5 to 8 minutes.

4. Serve with brown or wild rice.

MAKES 6 SERVINGS

PER SHISH KABOB	
CALORIES	190
PROTEIN	6.5 g
CARBOHYDRATES	13 g
FIBER	2 g
FAT	14 g
SODIUM	260 mg

Stuffed Mushrooms

Studies have revealed that some mushroom varieties have significant antioxidant qualities, the shiitake and mitake mushrooms in particular. In fact, history tells us that Chinese emperors consumed Shiitake mushrooms in large quantities to fend off old age. Portabella mushrooms are growing in popularity as well, but this recipe uses large white mushrooms, though others could be substituted. Served as an appetizer or entrée, stuffed mushrooms are a pleasant change from ordinary fare.

INGREDIENTS

1	pound	medium-sized mushrooms
1	tbsp	olive oil
1	stalk	celery, diced small
3½	ounces	firm tofu, diced
1	medium	zucchini, diced small*
1	medium	carrot, diced small
1½	cups	stuffing mix
2	tbsp	chopped fresh basil, *or*
1	tsp	dried basil
⅔	cup	water

GLAZE:

½ 1	cup + tbsp	water
1	tsp	Bragg Liquid Aminos
2	tsp	cornstarch
¼	tsp	onion powder
¼	tsp	garlic powder

Chopped broccoli stems may be substituted.

STEPS

1. Remove the stems from the mushrooms and chop fine. Reserve the caps.

2. Heat the olive oil in a large, heavy-bottomed skillet over a medium heat. Add the chopped mushroom stems, celery, tofu, zucchini, and carrot and cook for 3 to 4 minutes, stirring occasionally.

3. While vegetables are steaming, combine all glaze ingredients in a small saucepan and whisk to mix thoroughly. Cook glaze over medium-high heat until thickened. Set aside.

4. Stir the bread crumbs and chopped basil into the vegetable mixture. Add salt to taste and mix thoroughly.

5. Spoon the mixture into the mushroom caps. Pour the glaze into a shallow ovenproof dish and tilt to coat the bottom. Place the mushrooms in the dish on top of the glaze.

6. Bake in preheated oven at 425°F for 20 minutes, or until cooked through.

MAKES 8 SERVINGS

PER 2 MUSHROOMS	
CALORIES	170
PROTEIN	7 g
CARBOHYDRATES	25 g
FIBER	2.5 g
FAT	4.5 g
SODIUM	550 mg

Holiday Loaf

Though it resembles stuffing, this recipe is too good to be served on the side!

COOK'S TIP

A serving suggestion is to alternate **Baked Tofu**, *page 87,* slices with scoops of Holiday Loaf in a casserole dish. Bake as above and serve with **Herb Gravy,** *page 101.*

INGREDIENTS

2	cups	hearty whole-grain bread
2	cups	cooked brown rice
½	cup	chopped walnuts
1		green pepper, chopped
2	stalks	celery, diced
¼	cup	rinsed, raw cashews
1	cup	water
1	cup	minced onion
2	tbsp	Bragg Liquid Aminos
½	tsp	salt
1	tbsp	parsley flakes
1	tsp	sage

STEPS

1. Combine bread cubes, rice, walnuts, celery, pepper, and onion in a large bowl.

2. Blend cashews and water until smooth. Add to dry ingredients. Add seasoning and mix well.

3. Press into oiled loaf pans or small casserole dish. Bake covered 45 minutes at 350°F. Bake uncovered for an additional 15 to 20 minutes.

4. If slicing is desired, allow to cool completely, slice, and arrange on ovenproof platter, then reheat 15 to 20 minutes at 300°F.

MAKES 8 SERVINGS

PER ¾ CUP	
CALORIES	270
PROTEIN	9.5 g
CARBOHYDRATES	38 g
FIBER	6 g
FAT	11 g
SODIUM	690 mg

"The Lord God planted a garden. . . . And out of the ground the Lord God made every tree grow that is pleasant to the sight and good for food." —GENESIS 2:8, 9, NKJV

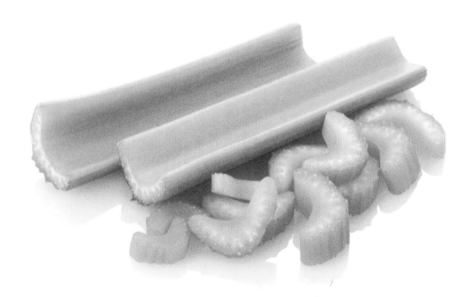

Millet Loaf

A small, round, yellow grain, millet packs a powerful nutritional punch. With more protein, B vitamins, iron, and copper than whole wheat, it is also a rich source of phosphorus. Millet has a subtle, nutlike flavor and is the only grain that is alkaline- and gluten-free.

INGREDIENTS

½	cup	raw cashews
1	cup	water
1	cup	wheat germ *or* bread crumbs
1½	cups	cooked millet
½	cup	quick oats
1	medium	onion, chopped
1	tbsp	chicken-style seasoning
½	tsp	garlic powder
2	tbsp	Bragg Liquid Aminos *or* soy sauce
½	tsp	sage

PER ⅛ LOAF	
CALORIES	165
PROTEIN	5.5 g
CARBOHYDRATES	20.5 g
FIBER	2 g
FAT	7.5 g
SODIUM	495 mg

STEPS

1. Blend cashews and water until smooth.
2. Combine well with remaining ingredients in a mixing bowl.
3. Pack into oil-sprayed loaf pan or casserole dish. Bake at 350°F for 25 to 30 minutes.
4. Patties can also be formed and browned in a nonstick skillet.
5. Serve with gravy for a formal meal, or this loaf makes an excellent sandwich filling with lettuce, tomato, and **Tofu Mayonnaise,** *page 63.*

MAKES 8 SERVINGS

COOK'S TIP

To prepare cooked millet, bring 3 cups of water and 1 cup of millet to a boil in a medium saucepan. Reduce heat to low, cover, and simmer for 30 minutes. Add a sprinkle of salt to serve as is for a breakfast cereal or use it in recipes. This will yield 3½ cups of cooked millet. It freezes well for future use.

Baked Tofu

A great chicken substitute, this tofu recipe is extremely quick, very tasty, and can be served as an entrée or used in other recipes. Serve with stuffing and gravy for an excellent holiday entrée.

INGREDIENTS

14	ounces	fresh, firm tofu
1	tbsp	chicken-style seasoning
¾	cup	water
2	tbsp	Bragg Liquid Aminos
2	tbsp	nutritional yeast

PER 2 SLICES	
CALORIES	125
PROTEIN	14 g
CARBOHYDRATES	5 g
FIBER	3 g
FAT	7 g
SODIUM	215 mg

STEPS

1. Cut tofu into slices ¼-inch thick (10 slices).
2. Mix remaining ingredients in a bowl and sprinkle over tofu.
3. Bake uncovered at 350°F for 30 to 40 minutes or until beginning to dry out a bit.

MAKES 10 SLICES

Crockpot Beans

Using the crockpot to cook beans is the absolute simplest way to prepare them. Split peas and lentils cook quickly and are best cooked on top of the stove; I use the crockpot for all other legumes. Add a little seasoning and serve them as they are or incorporate them into your favorite recipes.

INGREDIENTS

3	cups	dry beans
9	cups	water
1–2	tsp	salt, to taste
2	tsp	onion powder
½	tsp	garlic powder

STEPS

1 Sort beans on a dry dish towel, removing shriveled or discolored beans, as well as any foreign matter (rocks, etc.).

2 Wash beans in colander and place in a crockpot with water. Cook on low overnight or on high for 5 hours.

3 Add salt and other seasonings after beans are cooked.

MAKES 8 CUPS

PER ½ CUP	
CALORIES	118
PROTEIN	8 g
CARBOHYDRATES	21 g
FIBER	5 g
FAT	.5 g
SODIUM	300 mg

Vegetable Stir-fry

Tofu or Soy Curls make great additions to the veggies you choose to include in this Asian favorite. Keep some cooked brown rice on hand in the freezer to quickly thaw and heat for a complete meal.

COOK'S TIP

For additional protein, add seasoned tofu or Soy Curls.

INGREDIENTS

1		red bell pepper, cut into strips
1	medium	onion, cut into strips
1	can	sliced water chestnuts
2	medium	carrots, sliced
2	stalks	celery, sliced
2	cups	broccoli florets *or* asparagus
½	cup	toasted slivered almonds
1	cup	**Oriental Glaze,** *page 105*

STEPS

1 Steam carrots and celery for 5 minutes in large skillet with lid in ½ cup water. Add onions and continue steaming for 3 minutes.

2 Add broccoli and red bell pepper and steam an additional 3 minutes.

3 Add drained water chestnuts and toasted almonds.

4 Pour off any remaining water. Add **Oriental Glaze** and serve over brown rice.

MAKES 6 SERVINGS

PER 1 SERVING	
CALORIES	165
PROTEIN	5.5 g
CARBOHYDRATES	17 g
FIBER	5.5 g
FAT	10 g
SODIUM	215 mg

Best Oat Burgers

Moist and delicious, these are the best I've tasted. With lettuce, tomato, and mayonnaise on a quality whole-wheat bun, no one will be wondering where the beef went!

COOK'S TIP

Any leftover burgers can be frozen for later use. LaChoy Lite Soy Sauce may be substituted for the Bragg Liquid Aminos.

INGREDIENTS

4½	cups	water
¼	cup	Bragg Liquid Aminos
3	tbsp	olive oil
4½	cups	old-fashioned oats
1	cup	pecan meal
2	tsp	onion powder
½	tsp	garlic powder
1	tsp	salt
1	tsp	basil

STEPS

1. Bring water, Bragg Liquid Aminos, and olive oil to boil in a large saucepan.

2. Add oats and simmer for 10 minutes. Remove from heat. Add remaining ingredients and mix well.

3. Allow to cool just slightly and form into patties on oil-sprayed cookie sheet, using a round ¼-cup measure or ice-cream scoop to make uniform patties. With wet fingers, flatten patties and round edges.

4. Bake at 350°F for 30 to 35 minutes.

MAKES 20 BURGERS

PER BURGER	
CALORIES	190
PROTEIN	7 g
CARBOHYDRATES	24 g
FIBER	4.5 g
FAT	9 g
SODIUM	165 mg

Variation: For breakfast sausage, add 1½ teaspoon sage.

Soy Curls with Coconut Lime Sauce

A taste of the Caribbean right here at home!

INGREDIENTS

1½	cups	dry Soy Curls*
3	cups	water
2	tbsp	chicken-style seasoning
1	medium	onion, sliced
13.5-oz can		coconut milk
1	tbsp	cornstarch
2	tbsp	lime juice
		salt to taste

*Strips of **Baked Tofu,** page 87, can be substituted for the Soy Curls.

PER SERVING	
CALORIES	300
PROTEIN	7.5 g
CARBOHYDRATES	14.6 g
FIBER	4 g
FAT	19 g
SODIUM	426 mg

STEPS

1. Place Soy Curls, water, and 1 tablespoon of the chicken-style seasoning in a medium saucepan. Bring to a boil, then remove it from the heat.

2. In a skillet, steam the onion with a small amount of water until tender.

3. Drain the Soy Curls and add them to the skillet. Add the additional tablespoon of chicken-style seasoning and the coconut milk and bring the mixture to a boil.

4. Mix the cornstarch and the lime juice in a small bowl and add to the skillet, stirring until the sauce is thickened. It will thicken more as it cools.

5. Serve with brown rice and garnish with chopped scallions if desired.

MAKES 4 SERVINGS

Variations: Add steamed slivers of green and red bell pepper for a beautiful dish. This recipe is also delicious made with lemon juice instead of lime juice.

Garden Burgers

The ingredients for burgers with this name could vary as much as do vegetables from the garden. This version is delicious, but you might want to experiment with whatever vegetables you have on hand.

INGREDIENTS

½	cup	finely chopped onion
½	cup	grated carrots
⅓	cup	chopped black olives
2	cups	cooked brown rice
2	tbsp	flaxseed meal
1	tbsp	olive oil
2	tbsp	tomato purée
2	tsp	nutritional yeast flakes
1	tsp	onion powder
1	clove	fresh garlic, pressed
2	tsp	parsley flakes
1	tsp	basil
¾	tsp	salt

STEPS

1 Combine all ingredients in a bowl and mix well. Let stand just a few minutes to absorb liquid.

2 Form round flat patties on nonstick cookie sheet. Bake at 350°F for 35 to 40 minutes or until beginning to brown on the bottom.

MAKES 8 BURGERS

PER BURGER	
CALORIES	90
PROTEIN	2 g
CARBOHYDRATES	13 g
FIBER	2.2 g
FAT	4 g
SODIUM	475 mg

COOK'S TIP

Short of time, simply press entire recipe into an oil-sprayed loaf pan, cover, and bake at 350°F for 45 to 50 minutes. Remove cover for last 10 minutes. Cool slightly before slicing.

Sweet & Sour Soy Curls

Preparation of this tasty dish is quick and easy as no prehydrating is necessary. In a matter of minutes, dinner will be on the table!

INGREDIENTS

1	tbsp	olive oil *or* water
1		onion, chopped
1		bell pepper, sliced in 1-inch slices
4½	cups	Soy Curls
3½	cups	water
2	tbsp	Bragg Liquid Aminos *or* soy sauce
1½	tbsp	brown sugar *or* Sucanat
½	tsp	salt
1	tbsp	lemon juice
2	tbsp	nutritional yeast flakes

STEPS

1. Steam or sauté onion and pepper in a large skillet until tender.

2. Add Soy Curls and water and bring to a boil. Reduce heat, cover, and simmer for 5 minutes.

3. Add seasonings and stir well. Simmer an additional 5 minutes, stirring occasionally.

4. Serve immediately over brown rice.

MAKES 8 SERVINGS

PER SERVING	
CALORIES	135
PROTEIN	11.5 g
CARBOHYDRATES	10 g
FIBER	4.5 g
FAT	6.5 g
SODIUM	315 mg

HEALTH TIP

Meat, cheese, and all other animal products are completely devoid of fiber, a vital nutrient that plays a critical role in controlling weight and blood sugar, as well as in preventing colon cancer.

Zucchini Stacks

The perfect recipe for those zucchini that grow to a foot long overnight! Don't choose the extremely large ones, as the seeds might be tough. Three inches in diameter at the largest point is just right, and these stacked veggies are just delicious.

INGREDIENTS

1	medium	onion, diced
⅓	package	Gimme Lean mock sausage
1	tsp	each oregano, coriander, and cumin
28-oz can		whole, peeled plum tomatoes, drained; or 3 cups peeled, fresh tomato wedges
1	tbsp	olive oil
1	large	zucchini
2	tbsp	fresh parsley *or* basil, chopped

STEPS

1. Steam onion in small amount of water in large skillet.

2. As it is steaming, add mock sausage and break up into pieces with spatula. Cook until the onion is tender.

3. Add seasoning, oil, and tomatoes, breaking up tomatoes somewhat. If using fresh tomatoes, salt to taste.

4. Slice zucchini into ⅜-inch slices. Arrange the four largest ones on the bottom of an 8" x 8" baking dish.

5. Spoon the sauce over each slice, top with the next slices, add more sauce and continue with smaller slices and more sauce, three layers high.

6. Top stacks with chopped parsley or basil.

7. Bake for 30 to 40 minutes at 375°F. Serve with pasta and additional sauce.

MAKES 4 SERVINGS

PER STACK	
CALORIES	117
PROTEIN	8 g
CARBOHYDRATES	15 g
FIBER	3.5 g
FAT	4 g
SODIUM	380 mg

Pineapple Breakfast Pudding

It was an adult who reminded me to include this recipe, but the kids love it!

INGREDIENTS

1	cup	fresh pineapple chunks
⅓	cup	almonds
1		fresh pear, cored and quartered
12.3 ounces		firm, silken tofu
¼	cup	pitted dates
¼	tsp	salt

PER ½ CUP	
CALORIES	130
PROTEIN	6 g
CARBOHYDRATES	16 g
FIBER	3G
FAT	6 g
SODIUM	120 mg

STEPS

1 Blend all ingredients until smooth.

2 Serve with granola or Grape-Nuts, and fresh fruit.

MAKES 6 SERVINGS

Fruity Oatmeal

Choose your favorite fruit to add to the hot oatmeal. Fruity bursts of flavor provide a change of pace from this traditional favorite. Adding a banana makes it taste like warm banana pudding!

COOK'S TIP

If using apples or pears, add during last 10 minutes so the fruit cooks somewhat. Berries, mango, papaya, and banana may be added at the end.

INGREDIENTS

1	cup	old-fashioned oats
¼	tsp	salt
1¾	cups	water
1		banana, peach, pear, or berries

PER 1¼ CUP	
CALORIES	355
PROTEIN	13.8 g
CARBOHYDRATES	65.5 g
FIBER	9.8 g
FAT	5.6 g
SODIUM	297 mg

STEPS

1 Prepare oatmeal by bringing water and salt to a boil. Add oats and stir. Cover and reduce heat to low and simmer for 20 minutes.

2 Prepare fruit by chopping or slicing it into small chunks.

3 Just before serving, add sliced fruit, stir, and keep on low heat for one minute.

4 Serve with soymilk and top with nuts or granola if desired.

MAKES 2 SERVINGS

"I no longer recommend dairy products after the age of 2 years." —DR. BENJAMIN SPOCK,

PERHAPS THE MOST INFLUENTIAL PEDIATRICIAN OF ALL TIME, IN THE SEVENTH EDITION OF HIS WORLD-FAMOUS BOOK *BABY AND CHILD CARE.*

Pita Pizza

Plan a pizza bar and let everyone make their own so they can "have it their way." Throw the leftover fixings into the salad and you've got a party!

INGREDIENTS

1	package	whole-wheat pita bread; **Spaghetti Sauce,** *page 99,* or pizza sauce
		Quick & Easy Cheese, *page 62*

Topping ideas: Diced tomatoes, chopped onions, garlic, peppers, sliced black olives, **Best Oat Burger** *crumbles,* page 89, *zucchini, yellow squash*

PER PIZZA	
CALORIES	260
PROTEIN	13 g
CARBOHYDRATES	37 g
FIBER	8.5 g
FAT	9.5 g
SODIUM	1135 mg

STEPS

1. Spread sauce on pita bread. Top with toppings of your choice.

2. Spoon cheese on top. **Healthy Melty Cheese,** *page 103,* or a commercial soy mozzarella can be used.

3. Sprinkle with Italian seasonings and finish with sliced black olives.

4. Bake at 400°F directly on oven rack for 10 minutes. Serve immediately.

MAKES 8 SERVINGS

"Oh, give thanks to the Lord, for He is good! For His mercy endures forever." —PSALM 107:1, NKJV

Zucchini Patties

Nobody said they're crab cakes, but with a little tartar sauce, I begin to hear the waves lapping. Well, OK, you try it!

INGREDIENTS

1	cup	**Tofu Mayonnaise,** *page 63*
2–3	cups	hearty, whole-grain bread crumbs
½	tsp	garlic powder
1	tsp	Bragg Liquid Aminos
3	cups	shredded zucchini*
1	tsp	salt
½	tsp	ground bay leaves
½	tsp	marjoram
½	tsp	kelp (optional)
1	tbsp	parsley flakes

PER 1 PATTY	
CALORIES	210
PROTEIN	14.5 g
CARBOHYDRATES	24.5 g
FIBER	7 g
FAT	6.5 g
SODIUM	530 mg

COOK'S TIP

Commercial breadcrumbs can be used, but homemade bread crumbs are easily made by grinding **Whole-Wheat Bread,** *page 55,* in a food processor and adding garlic powder and a sprinkle of Italian seasonings.

STEPS

1. Combine all ingredients in a large bowl and mix well.

2. Spoon into a preheated nonstick skillet, forming patties with the back of the spoon.

3. Cook 10 minutes on each side.

MAKES 12 PATTIES

Squeeze juice out of zucchini after shredding. The amount of bread crumbs needed will depend on the juiciness of the zucchini.

Easy-Peasy

Let the kids help you make this recipe.

INGREDIENTS

4	medium	baking potatoes
1	cup	frozen peas
1	cup	**Herb Gravy,** *page 101*
		salt to taste

STEPS

1 Pierce the potatoes with a fork and bake them at 350°F for 1 hour.

2 Scoop out the potato into a bowl, leaving ¼ inch of potato next to the skin. Mash the potato with the **Herb Gravy** to a chunky filling. Add the peas and mix. Add salt to taste.

3 Stuff the potato shells with the filling, and place on a baking sheet.

4 Bake at 350°F for 20 minutes. Broil the last 1 minute to brown slightly.

MAKES 8 HALVES

PER SERVING	
CALORIES	125
PROTEIN	3.5 g
CARBOHYDRATES	21.5 g
FIBER	4 g
FAT	3 g
SODIUM	155 mg

Trail Mix

Whether you're hitting the trail or just having a picnic, this low-fat variety is a hit with kids of all ages!

INGREDIENTS

1	cup	Cheerios
½	cup	walnuts
½	cup	sunflower seeds
¾	cup	Spoon Size Shredded Wheat
½	cup	carob chips
¾	cup	raisins

STEPS

1 Combine all ingredients in a large bowl and serve.

2 If making ahead, omit the raisins and store in a plastic bag. Add raisins just before serving.

MAKES 8 SERVINGS

PER ½ CUP	
CALORIES	210
PROTEIN	5 g
CARBOHYDRATES	25 g
FIBER	3 g
FAT	11 g
SODIUM	470 mg

Alphabet Soup

The kids will spell "Thank you" when they find this fun soup in their bowl. Make it quickly with frozen or canned vegetables.

INGREDIENTS

1	small	onion, chopped
1	stalk	celery, sliced
1	can	whole tomatoes
1	medium	potato, diced
1		carrot, diced
3	cups	water
2	tsp	chicken-style seasoning
½	cup	corn
½	cup	peas
¼	cup	whole-wheat alphabet noodles

STEPS

1 Steam onion, garlic, and celery in a small amount of water or sauté in olive oil.

2 Add tomatoes, potatoes, carrots, water, and chicken-style seasoning. Bring to a boil and simmer for 15 minutes

3 Add corn, peas, and alphabet noodles and continue cooking for 10 minutes.

MAKES 8 SERVINGS

PER 1 CUP	
CALORIES	75
PROTEIN	2.5 g
CARBOHYDRATES	16.5 g
FIBER	3 g
FAT	.5 g
SODIUM	275 mg

Banana Popsicles

Better have some of these in the freezer when the grandkids come to visit. Let them in on the fun and get them to help make them.

INGREDIENTS

2		ripe bananas
1	recipe	**Carob Fudge Sauce,** *page 112*
4		Popsicle sticks
¾	cup	chopped nuts *or* toasted coconut

PER POPSICLE	
CALORIES	320
PROTEIN	6 g
CARBOHYDRATES	42.5 g
FIBER	5.5 g
FAT	17 g
SODIUM	105 mg

STEPS

1 Peel bananas and cut in half. Insert Popsicle stick and dip into **Carob Fudge Sauce,** coating completely.

2 Roll gently in chopped nuts or toasted coconut.

3 Freeze on plate covered with waxed paper. Allow to thaw just slightly before serving.

MAKES 4 POPSICLES

Variation: For frozen *Carob Bon Bons,* use ½-inch banana slices instead of half a banana. Dip slices then freeze them on a waxed paper-covered plate or cookie sheet. Store in a plastic bag.

"Taste and see that the Lord is good!" —PSALM 34:8, NKJV

Quinoa Pilaf

Gluten-free and high in fiber, quinoa (kween'-wa) has a balanced essential amino acid profile, making it a complete protein source. High in magnesium and iron, it's considered a superfood. Besides that, it's super good in recipes or by itself with a sprinle of salt and nutitional yeast flakes.

COOK'S TIP

Vary the veggies according to your preference; broccoli and red bell pepper, and edamame and yellow squash are good combinations. Think color; think nutrition.

INGREDIENTS

8	ounces	quinoa
3	cups	water
½	tsp	salt
1	cup	chopped onion
1	clove	fresh garlic, pressed
1	small	zucchini, diced
1		carrot, sliced
1	tbsp	olive oil
1	tbsp	Bragg Liquid Aminos
1	tsp	dried basil
1	tbsp	parsley flakes

STEPS

1. Cook quinoa according to package. Allow to cool.
2. Steam onion, garlic, zucchini, and carrot in a small amount of water in a large saucepan.
3. Add cooked rice and remaining ingredients and toss to mix.

MAKES 6 SERVINGS

PER ½ CUP	
CALORIES	130
PROTEIN	4.5 g
CARBOHYDRATES	23 g
FIBER	2 g
FAT	2.5 g
SODIUM	310 mg

Aussie Potato Bake

My Australian friend Robert was a guest in our home from time to time during his college days. He shared with me how he longed for potatoes like the ones his "mum" used to make. This is what he described and, sure enough, I think it took care of his homesickness, for that meal anyway! Now we all have "Mum's" recipe. It's exceptional!

INGREDIENTS

2	medium	sweet potatoes
2	medium	white potatoes
13.5-oz can		coconut milk
½	tsp	salt

STEPS

1. Peel and slice potatoes in rounds.
2. Layer in an 8" x 8" casserole dish, lightly sprinkling the layers with salt.
3. Pour the coconut milk over the potatoes.
4. Bake at 400°F for 45 minutes or until potatoes are tender.

MAKES 6 SERVINGS

PER SERVING	
CALORIES	210
PROTEIN	3 g
CARBOHYDRATES	20.5 g
FIBER	3 g
FAT	13.5 g
SODIUM	210 mg

"Nothing will benefit human health and increase chances of survival for life on earth as much as the evolution to a vegetarian diet." —ALBERT EINSTEIN

Oven-roasted Potatoes

Loaded with potassium, roasted potatoes are delicious with only salt, but even more so with these added ingredients.

INGREDIENTS

3	large	Russet potatoes *or*
5	medium	red potatoes
1	tbsp	olive oil
½	tsp	garlic powder
2	tbsp	Bragg Liquid Aminos *or*
1	tsp	salt
½	tsp	Italian seasonings *or*
1	tbsp	fresh rosemary
1	tsp	onion powder
½	tsp	paprika
2	tbsp	nutritional yeast flakes

STEPS

1. If using Russet potatoes, slice each potato into eight wedges and place them in a large casserole dish. Cut red potatoes into 1½-inch cubes.

2. Drizzle and sprinkle with remaining ingredients, then toss to coat potatoes.

3. Roast at 450°F for 30 minutes or until tender.

MAKES 6 SERVINGS

PER SERVING	
CALORIES	160
PROTEIN	4.5 g
CARBOHYDRATES	34 g
FIBER	2.5 g
FAT	1.5 g
SODIUM	230 mg

Roasted Root Vegetables

Roasting brings out the sweetness and rich flavor of these fall and winter veggies. Other vegetables can be roasted as well, or you can use a variation of those listed. Roasted vegetables are a wonderful addition to a holiday meal.

INGREDIENTS

2	medium	carrots
3	medium	parsnips
2	medium	turnips
2	medium	red potatoes
1	large	sweet potato
1	large	onion
½	tsp	salt
1	tbsp	olive oil
1	tsp	dried thyme

STEPS

1. Preheat oven to 450°F.

2. Peel and cut root vegetables into ¾-inch chunks. Spread single layer onto a large baking sheet.

3. Cut onion into chunks and separate into 2-layer pieces. Add to vegetables.

4. Drizzle vegetables with olive oil and sprinkle with salt and thyme.

5. Stir to coat well.

6. Roast uncovered for 45 minutes.

MAKES 12 SERVINGS

PER SERVING	
CALORIES	90
PROTEIN	2 g
CARBOHYDRATES	18 g
FIBER	3.5 g
FAT	1.5 g
SODIUM	125 mg

Eat for strength! —ECCLESIASTES 10:17

Cauliflower au Gratin

Your family will not believe this recipe has no cheese in it. It is reminiscent of a gruyere cheese casserole that I was served in France, and it is just as tasty. Tahini is the key ingredient that gives this dish a wonderful, cheesy flavor.

INGREDIENTS

1		head of cauliflower
2½	cups	water
¼	cup	rinsed, raw cashews
1	tbsp	lemon juice
¼	cup	nutritional yeast flakes
2	tbsp	tahini
1	tsp	onion powder
¼	tsp	garlic powder
¼	cup	cornstarch
1¼	tsp	salt
1	jar	pearl onions

STEPS

1. Core the cauliflower and cut it into 2-inch pieces, then place them in a large steamer. Steam until crisp tender.

2. Bring 1½ cups of the water to a boil in a saucepan.

3. Liquefy the remaining ingredients, and include the remaining 1 cup of water, in the blender.

4. Pour blended mixture into boiling water and continue cooking until thick.

5. Arrange cauliflower and pearl onions in a large casserole dish. Pour sauce over vegetables and serve. Garnish with fresh parsley and paprika.

MAKES 8 SERVINGS

PER SERVING	
CALORIES	130
PROTEIN	6 g
CARBOHYDRATES	16 g
FIBER	5 g
FAT	6 g
SODIUM	460 mg

Fresh Collard Greens

Collard, kale, and turnip greens are rich sources of calcium, as well as folate, and should be served at least weekly. No Southern meal is complete without them!

INGREDIENTS

10	cups	fresh collards
2	cups	water
1	tsp	onion powder
½	tsp	garlic powder
½	tsp	salt
		Bakon yeast (optional)

STEPS

1. Wash and chop desired amount of collards and place in a large saucepan with about 1½ inches of water in bottom of pan.

2. Bring to a boil over medium-high heat. Cover and reduce heat and simmer for 30 to 45 minutes or less, just until tender. It will depend on how tender the greens are.

3. Add seasonings. For those who enjoy a bacon-like seasoning, Bakon yeast, which is dried torula yeast with a hickory smoke flavor, can be added, but these greens are still very delicious with the simple ingredients included.

4. Serve with lemon juice, if desired.

MAKES 6 SERVINGS

HEALTH TIP

Dark-green leafy vegetables and prepared dried beans are excellent sources of calcium, the mineral that helps us build a strong skeletal system. Weight-bearing exercise also helps to strengthen the bones. Include walking, gardening, or other physical activity most days of the week to help keep your bones strong.

PER ½ CUP	
CALORIES	25
PROTEIN	2 g
CARBOHYDRATES	5 g
FIBER	2.5 g
FAT	.5 g
SODIUM	150 mg
CALCIUM	100 mg
FOLATE	100 mcg

Southern Side of

This is one vegetable I like "cooked to death." Please notice I have left out the bacon grease!

COOK'S TIP

Serve with fresh or frozen lima beans (known as "butter beans" in the South), cooked until tender, and with garden fresh tomatoes and corn on the cob.

INGREDIENTS

4	medium	yellow summer squash
1	large	onion
½	tsp	salt
1	tbsp	olive oil

STEPS

1. Slice squash into ¼-inch rounds and onion into half-rounds.
2. Coat the bottom of a large skillet with the olive oil. Add squash, onions, and salt and sauté for 5 minutes. Cover.
3. Turn down heat, allowing squash to simmer for about 30 minutes, until tender.
4. Chop squash and onions into ½- to 1-inch pieces with a firm spatula.
5. Continue cooking an additional 10 minutes.

MAKES 4 SERVINGS

PER SERVING	
CALORIES	70
PROTEIN	2.5 g
CARBOHYDRATES	10.5 g
FIBER	2.5 g
FAT	2.5 g
SODIUM	300 mg

Spaghetti Sauce

The secret to making classic Italian sauce is using crushed tomatoes. Purchase only an Italian brand for the desired texture. When you start with quality crushed tomatoes, arriving at an authentic sauce is simple.

COOK'S TIP

This recipe calls for diced tomatoes for the sake of convenience. I prefer whole tomatoes that you crush with your hands.

INGREDIENTS

1½	tsp	olive oil
1	cup	diced onion
2	cloves	garlic, pressed
28-oz can		crushed tomatoes
14.4-oz can		diced tomatoes
1	tsp	salt
1	tsp	basil
½	tsp	lemon juice
1	tsp	olive oil
½	tsp	oregano
1	tsp	honey

STEPS

1. Sauté onions and garlic in oil.
2. Add remaining ingredients and simmer for 10 minutes.

MAKES 6 CUPS

PER ½ CUP	
CALORIES	40
PROTEIN	1 g
CARBOHYDRATES	7 g
FIBER	1.5 g
FAT	1 g
SODIUM	350 mg

"Bless the Lord, O my soul" "Who satisfies your mouth with good things, so that your youth is renewed like the eagle's." —PSALM 103:1, 5, NKJV

Sweet Potato Soufflé

Not really a soufflé, this dish is a must-have at every Thanksgiving dinner. It is rich in beta-carotene and topped with walnuts, giving it a wonderful blend of taste and texture.

INGREDIENTS

4	medium	sweet potatoes
2	tsp	vanilla extract
2	tsp	honey
¼	tsp	salt
1	tsp	ground coriander
¼	cup	soy or nut milk
1	tbsp	molasses
¼	cup	walnuts, chopped

STEPS

1. Wash sweet potatoes and pierce with a fork.
2. Bake until soft and juices are appearing (350°F for about an hour).
3. Cool, peel, and mash sweet potatoes and add remaining ingredients. A food processor works well.
4. Pour into a casserole dish and top with chopped walnuts.
5. Bake at 350°F for 30 minutes.

MAKES 6 SERVINGS

PER ½ CUP	
CALORIES	95
PROTEIN	2 g
CARBOHYDRATES	16 g
FIBER	2.5 g
FAT	2.5 g
SODIUM	85 mg

HEALTH TIP

When we look at sweet potatoes, we see beta-carotene, but they are also good sources of calcium, potassium, and fiber. Sweet potato recipes made with healthful ingredients make the perfect side or dessert.

Fresh Cranberry Relish

Tangy and festive, this is the perfect accompaniment to a Thanksgiving dinner. Leftover relish makes a good topping for toast that has been spread with almond butter.

INGREDIENTS

3	cups	fresh cranberries
1	large	apple
6	large	dried apricots
½	cup	frozen white grape cranberry or white grape raspberry juice concentrate

STEPS

1. Process cranberries in food processor until chopped fine, then transfer to a mixing bowl.
2. Core and peel apple and then cut into chunks. Place in food processor and chop fine. Add to cranberries.
3. Use a knife to dice dried apricots into small pieces. Add to bowl.
4. Add remaining ingredients and mix well.
5. Serve chilled with a savory entrée for a festive holiday meal.

MAKES 8 SERVINGS

PER ¼ CUP	
CALORIES	65
PROTEIN	.5 g
CARBOHYDRATES	16 g
FIBER	3 g
FAT	0 g
SODIUM	2 mg

"By eating the right food, we can keep our hearts healthy." —T. COLIN CAMPBELL, PH.D.

Herb Gravy

For many, the best part of a "meat and potatoes" meal is the gravy, and this one is something to write home about. In addition, it can be used very successfully to replace butter and milk in mashed potatoes. Serve with **Millet Loaf,** *page 87,* or **Holiday Loaf,** *page 86,* for a special meal anytime of year.

INGREDIENTS

½	cup	rinsed, raw cashews
2	cups	water
4½	tsp	cornstarch
1½	tsp	onion powder
½	tsp	garlic powder
1½	tsp	Bragg Liquid Aminos
½	tsp	lemon juice
½	tsp	dried basil *or*
1	tbsp	fresh basil
	pinch	rosemary
½	tsp	salt
1	tsp	parsley flakes *or*
1	sprig	fresh parsley

STEPS

1. Bring 1 cup of the water to a boil in a medium saucepan.
2. Blend remaining ingredients, except parsley, until very smooth in the blender.
3. Pour blended mixture into the boiling water and stir with a whisk until thickened. The gravy will thicken further as it cools. Garnish with parsley.

MAKES 2½ CUPS

PER ¼ CUP	
CALORIES	70
PROTEIN	2 g
CARBOHYDRATES	4.5 g
FIBER	.5 g
FAT	5.5 g
SODIUM	150 mg

"Those who persevere in obedience to the laws of health will reap the reward in health of body and health of mind." —ELLEN G. WHITE

Pan-fried Okra

Another Southern favorite, but without the health risk of the deep-fried version or the dreaded "slime factor"!

INGREDIENTS

20		okra pods
½	cup	cornmeal
2	tbsp	whole-wheat flour
½	tsp	salt
2	tbsp	light olive oil

STEPS

1. Slice okra into ½-inch rounds.
2. Put okra and dry ingredients into a plastic bag and shake well to coat evenly.
3. Place in preheated skillet with the oil. Brown for 10 minutes over medium heat, turning with spatula every couple of minutes. Reduce heat, cover, and continue cooking for 5 more minutes, turning okra after 3 minutes.
4. Remove lid and continue browning until crisp, another 5 minutes. Serve hot.

MAKES 4 SERVINGS

PER SERVING	
CALORIES	145
PROTEIN	3 g
CARBOHYDRATES	18G
FIBER	2.5 g
FAT	7.5 g
SODIUM	300 mg

Onion Rings

Fried onion rings might naturally be vegetarian, but the damaging high fat will likely negate any benefit. This version is absolutely delicious and completely healthful. Eggplant can also be prepared in this manner as well. Serve it with tartar sauce.

INGREDIENTS

3	large	onions
1	recipe	**Tofu Mayonnaise,** *page 63*
3	cups	seasoned whole-grain bread crumbs

STEPS

1. Slice onions and separate into rings.
2. Thin out mayonnaise in a small bowl with a little water, about 2 tablespoons.
3. Dip onion rings in mayonnaise with one fork, then use another fork to place on a plateful of bread crumbs. Turn to coat evenly.
4. Bake on nonstick cookie sheet at 325°F for 20 to 25 minutes.

MAKES ABOUT 42

PER 6 ONION RINGS	
CALORIES	190
PROTEIN	12 g
CARBOHYDRATES	19 g
FIBER	4 g
FAT	8.5 g
SODIUM	375 mg

"Do you not know that your body is the temple of the Holy Spirit who is in you, whom you have from God, and you are not your own? For you were bought at a price; therefore glorify God in your body and in your Spirit, which are God's." —1 CORINTHIANS 6:19, 20, NKJV

Summer Squash Bake

Baking vegetables minimizes steps in the kitchen and maximizes nutrient retention. When the garden is producing squash and onions, this is perfect for a potluck.

INGREDIENTS

4	medium	summer squash
1	large	onion
1	recipe	**Healthy Melty Cheese,** *page 103*

STEPS

1. Preheat oven to 400°F.
2. Slice squash and onions and arrange in 9" x 13" casserole dish.
3. Pour **Healthy Melty Cheese** over vegetables.
4. Bake for 30 minutes.

MAKES 8 SERVINGS

PER SERVING	
CALORIES	130
PROTEIN	5.5 g
CARBOHYDRATES	16 g
FIBER	3.5 g
FAT	6 g
SODIUM	410 mg

Healthy Melty Cheese

This sauce so closely resembles the real thing, you can fool anybody. Considering that it is very low in fat and cholesterol free, it can be enjoyed often.

INGREDIENTS

¼	cup	rinsed, raw cashews
4-oz jar		pimiento, drained
1	tbsp	lemon juice
¼	cup	nutritional yeast flakes
2	tbsp	tahini
1	tsp	onion powder
¼	tsp	garlic powder
3	tbsp	cornstarch
1¼	tsp	salt
¼	tsp	celery seed (optional)
2½	cups	water

STEPS

1. Bring 1½ cups of the water to a boil in a saucepan.
2. Liquefy the remaining ingredients, include the remaining 1 cup of water in the blender until smooth.
3. Pour blended mixture into boiling water and continue cooking until thick.
4. Serve immediately over broccoli, pasta, baked potato, or toast, or you can use in a casserole.

MAKES 3 CUPS

PER ¼ CUP	
CALORIES	60
PROTEIN	2.5 g
CARBOHYDRATES	6 g
FIBER	1.5 g
FAT	3.5 g
SODIUM	250 mg

Italian Marinade

Perfect for grilled tofu or shish kabobs. Also is an excellent marinade for roasted vegetables.

INGREDIENTS

½	cup	olive oil
½	cup	water
⅓	cup	lemon juice
4	tsp	honey
1	tbsp	Bragg Liquid Aminos
2	tsp	parsley flakes
2	large	cloves pressed garlic
1	tsp	onion powder
½	tsp	oregano
¼	tsp	salt

STEPS

1. Combine all ingredients in a jar and shake to mix, or pulse briefly in the blender.
2. Marinate tofu, vegetables, or reconstituted Soy Curls for about 30 minutes before grilling, broiling, or roasting.

MAKES 1½ CUPS

COOK'S TIP

If using the blender to mix, pressing the garlic cloves will be unnecessary.

PER 2 TABLESPOONS	
CALORIES	65
PROTEIN	.5 g
CARBOHYDRATES	3 g
FIBER	.1 g
FAT	6 g
SODIUM	100 mg

Béarnaise Sauce

Usually considered a sauce for meat, this béarnaise sauce is a wonderful accompaniment for **Baked Tofu**, *page 87*, or steamed vegetables.

INGREDIENTS

2	tbsp	light olive oil
2	tbsp	white flour
1	cup	plain soymilk
1	tbsp	lemon juice
½	tsp	onion powder
¼	tsp	garlic powder
$\frac{1}{16}$	tsp	turmeric
¼	tsp	salt

PER 2 TABLESPOONS	
CALORIES	45
PROTEIN	1 g
CARBOHYDRATES	2.5 g
FIBER	.5 g
FAT	3.5 g
SODIUM	70 mg

STEPS

1 Heat oil over medium heat in a saucepan. Add flour and stir to make a roux (paste).

2 Gradually add milk, stirring constantly over heat to avoid lumping.

3 Add remaining ingredients and continue to stir until smooth. Serve immediately.

MAKES A LITTLE OVER 1 CUP

COOK'S TIP

If preferred, all ingredients can be combined in the blender. Whiz for 15 seconds, then cook on medium heat until thick, stirring constantly.

Spanish Rice

Another authentic recipe from Zinia, the flavor achieved warrants the effort.

INGREDIENTS

1	cup	fresh *or* frozen corn
½	cup	red *and/or* green pepper, chopped
1	medium	onion, diced
½	cup	fresh cilantro, chopped
2-3	cloves	garlic, thinly sliced
2-3	tsp	tomato paste *or* purée
2-3	tsp	olive oil
3	cups	short grain brown rice
5½	cups	water
1½	tsp	salt

PER ½ CUP	
CALORIES	150
PROTEIN	3.5 g
CARBOHYDRATES	30 g
FIBER	3 g
FAT	2 g
SODIUM	240 mg

STEPS

1 In a large, heavy-bottom saucepan, sauté corn, pepper, onion, cilantro, garlic, and tomato paste in the olive oil.

2 Add rice, water, and salt.

3 Cover and cook for 45 minutes on low heat. Gently fluff with a fork.

MAKES 16 SERVINGS

COOK'S TIP

Here's a shortcut method: Sauté ingredients in step number 1. Add 4 cups cooked brown rice. Salt to taste and add more tomato purée if desired. Mix well and heat through. Quick and easy!

Oriental Glaze

This glaze is the finishing touch to an Asian vegetable stir-fry. Adjust the Bragg to your liking and your sodium requirements.

INGREDIENTS

2	cups	water *or* pineapple juice
¼	cup	cornstarch
¼	cup	Bragg Liquid Aminos
1	tsp	garlic powder *or*
2	cloves	sliced fresh garlic
1	tsp	lemon juice (optional)

STEPS

1 Pour 1½ cups water or juice in medium saucepan and bring to boil.

2 Mix remaining ½ cup water or juice with the other ingredients in a cup or small bowl.

3 Add cornstarch mixture to boiling liquid. Stir constantly with whisk until thickened.

4 Pour over steamed vegetables and mix for **Vegetable Stir-fry,** *page 88.*

MAKES 2½ CUPS

PER ¼ CUP (USING PINEAPPLE JUICE)

CALORIES	45
PROTEIN	.5 g
CARBOHYDRATES	10.5 g
FIBER	.2 g
FAT	0 g
SODIUM	260 mg

Picadillo Sauce

A fancy salsa straight from Puerto Rico.

COOK'S TIP

If serving with burritos, garnish the dish with sliced black olives and shredded soy cheese.

INGREDIENTS

½	cup	chopped onion
½	cup	chopped green pepper
1	stalk	celery, finely diced
½	cup	fresh cilantro leaves, sliced thin
1	tsp	garlic powder
½	tsp	cumin
1	cup	canned diced tomatoes
	pinch	salt
1	tsp	sweetener
1	tsp	cornstarch
½	cup	water

STEPS

1 In large skillet, sauté onion, green pepper, and cilantro leaves in oil or cover and steam in water just until tender.

2 Add garlic powder, cumin, tomatoes, and sweetener to the sautéed vegetables and bring to a boil.

3 Dissolve cornstarch in the water, pour into the vegetable mixture.

4 Reduce heat and continue cooking for 2 to 3 minutes, stirring constantly until thickened. Serve hot over burritos.

MAKES 3 CUPS

PER ¼ CUP

CALORIES	25
PROTEIN	.5 g
CARBOHYDRATES	3.5 g
FIBER	.5 g
FAT	1 g
SODIUM	50 mg

Banana Date

These cookies are naturally sweet and delicious, and they are especially good right out of the oven and cooled just a bit.

INGREDIENTS

3		ripe bananas, mashed
1	cup	chopped dates
½	cup	walnuts, chopped
2	cups	quick oats
1	cup	unsweetened coconut
1	cup	raisins
1	tsp	vanilla extract
½	tsp	salt

PER COOKIE	
CALORIES	170
PROTEIN	2.5 g
CARBOHYDRATES	21.5 g
FIBER	3.5 g
FAT	9 g
SODIUM	55 mg

STEPS

1 Preheat oven to 350°F.

2 Mash bananas with a fork on a plate. Combine with all ingredients in a mixing bowl and mix well.

3 Drop by tablespoons onto nonstick cookie sheet. Flatten with a fork and bake for 25 minutes.

MAKES 24 COOKIES

COOK'S TIP

These are best served within several hours from the oven. The next day, reheat to crisp before serving.

"Drugs and surgery don't cure the diseases that kill most Americans." —T. COLIN CAMPBELL, PH.D.

Happy Cookies

Chock-full of omega-3 essential fatty acid, these delicious cookies might even aid in lifting depression! See Dr. Neil Nedley's book, **Depression: The Way Out,** for a complete lifestyle program designed to combat depression.

COOK'S TIP

Raisins are a wonderful substitute for the carob chips, or get creative and add other chopped dried fruits.

INGREDIENTS

2½	cups	English walnuts
⅔	cup	maple syrup
1	tbsp	light olive oil
2	tsp	vanilla extract
1	tsp	salt
⅓	cup	flax meal
½	cup	whole-wheat flour
⅓	cup	dairy-free carob chips

STEPS

1. Preheat oven to 350°F.

2. Grind 1½ cups of the walnuts in the blender or food processor, leaving some coarsely ground. Pour into a mixing bowl.

3. Blend remaining 1 cup of walnuts with the maple syrup, oil, vanilla extract, and salt in a blender. Mixture should be smooth and creamy.

4. Add blended mixture to the ground walnuts. Add remaining ingredients and mix well.

5. Form cookies by placing slightly more than 1 tablespoon of batter on nonstick cookie sheet. Flatten with the back of a spoon coated with oil. (Using a small scoop sprayed with oil also works well.)

6. Bake for 12 minutes. Watch closely as oven temperatures can vary.

PER 1 COOKIE	
CALORIES	140
PROTEIN	2.5 g
CARBOHYDRATES	11.5 g
FIBER	10 g
FAT	10 g
SODIUM	100 mg

MAKES 24 COOKIES

Carob Brownies

Looking for a gluten-free brownie? Substituting brown rice flour works perfectly. In fact, it creates a chewier brownie. Yum! It's perfect for hot fudge cake, using Tofutti or homemade vegan ice cream, of course!

COOK'S TIP

For an excellent pudding topping, crumble several brownies and spread onto cookie sheet. Crisp in 250° oven for 20 minutes.

INGREDIENTS

⅔	cup	whole-wheat flour
½	cup	carob powder
1	tbsp	powdered coffee substitute (Roma)
⅓	cup	Sucanat *or* brown sugar
1	tbsp	Ener-G baking powder *or*
1½	tsp	Rumford baking powder
1	cup	walnuts, chopped
¾	cup	soy *or* nut milk
½	tsp	salt
1	tsp	vanilla extract
⅓	cup	honey

STEPS

1. Preheat oven to 400°F. Prepare 8" x 8" pan with nonstick spray.

2. Measure all dry ingredients, except walnuts, into one bowl and wet ingredients into another. Add walnuts to wet ingredients.

3. When oven is hot, mix together dry and wet ingredients. Stir quickly, being careful not to stir out bubbles. (Ener-G baking powder is moisture activated, while Rumford is heat activated.) Place in oven immediately.

4. Bake at 400°F for 5 minutes, then reduce heat to 350°F and continue baking for 25 minutes. Cool and top with **Carob Fudge Sauce,** *page 112.*

PER BROWNIE	
CALORIES	235
PROTEIN	4 g
CARBOHYDRATES	38 g
FIBER	3.2 g
FAT	9 g
SODIUM	150 mg

MAKES 9 LARGE BROWNIES

Pineapple Right-Side-Up Cake

Here is a recipe with quite a few steps, but it's easy to get it right! A luscious, creamy combination, this cake will get rave reviews.

INGREDIENTS

CAKE:

1	cup	whole-wheat flour
1	cup	unbleached white flour
2	tbsp	Ener-G baking powder *or*
1	tbsp	Rumford baking powder
¾	tsp	salt
½	cup	light olive oil
½	cup	honey
1	cup	pineapple juice
1	tsp	vanilla extract
½	tsp	coconut extract

TOPPING:

6	ounces	silken tofu, extra firm
13.5-oz can		coconut milk
3	tbsp	sweetener
⅛	tsp	salt
1	tsp	vanilla extract
2	tsp	Instant Clear Jel

To assemble, you will also need:

20-oz can		crushed pineapple, in juice
⅓	cup	toasted slivered almonds
¼	cup	diced dried apricots

STEPS

CAKE:

1. Preheat oven to 375°F.
2. Combine flours, baking powder, and salt in a medium bowl and stir with a whisk.
3. Combine remaining liquid ingredients in another bowl and mix well.
4. Pour liquid mixture over dry ingredients and mix well, being careful not to stir bubbles out.
5. Bake in oiled and floured 9-inch round pan for 45 minutes.

TOPPING:

6. Place all ingredients, except Instant Clear Jel, in blender. Blend until smooth.
7. Sprinkle Instant Clear Jel into blender while blending mixture on medium speed. Chill for 2 to 3 hours, until thick.
8. Drain ½ cup juice from the pineapple.
9. Spoon pineapple over cake, allowing some juice to penetrate the cake.
10. Top with coconut milk topping, toasted almonds, and apricots.

MAKES 12 SERVINGS

PER SERVING	
CALORIES	425
PROTEIN	8.5 g
CARBOHYDRATES	54 g
FIBER	4 g
FAT	21.5 g
SODIUM	215 mg

German Carob Cake

Did you ever feel like you were "going international" when serving German chocolate cake? Turns out, a homemaker in Dallas, Texas, developed the recipe— and its name comes from the sweet chocolate baking bar developed for Baker's Chocolate Company in 1852 by Sam German. For most of us, it's the frosting that is the signature trait of this old favorite, and this version is delicious without the butter, eggs, and milk. Walnuts are used instead of pecans as they maintain a crispier texture. The carob cake recipe is a great stand-in for the German chocolate cake. Carob is already sweet, like Mr. German's chocolate bar, so it's the perfect healthy alternative. This cake is rich, so serve it with a meal that is lower in fat.

COOK'S TIP

This cake is also excellent with **Carob Fudge Sauce,** *page 112,* or **Berry Fruit Sauce,** *page 112;* or to make Black Forest Cake, layer with **Carob Mocha Mousse,** *page 114;* fresh, pitted dark cherries; and frost with **Coconut Whipped Cream,** *page 113.*

INGREDIENTS

CAKE:

3⅓	cups	whole-wheat pastry flour
2	tbsp	Ener-G baking powder *or*
1	tbsp	Rumford baking powder
2	cups	Sucanat or turbinado sugar
1	tsp	salt
6	tbsp	carob powder
1	tbsp	powdered coffee substitute (Roma)
⅔	cup	unrefined light olive oil
2	cups	water
2	tsp	vanilla extract

COCONUT WALNUT FROSTING:

2	cups	vanilla soy milk
½	cup	Sucanat
½	cup	chopped dates
1	tsp	vanilla extract
¼	tsp	salt
4	tsp	cornstarch
2	cups	unsweetened, flake coconut
1	cup	English walnuts, coarsely chopped

STEPS

CAKE:

1. Preheat oven to 350°F.

2. Mix dry ingredients in one bowl and wet ingredients in another.

3. Combine liquid to dry ingredients and mix until moist and most lumps have disappeared.

4. Pour into two 9-inch cake pans and bake immediately. Bake until toothpick inserted in center comes out clean, 35 to 40 minutes.

FROSTING:

5. Blend all ingredients, except the coconut and walnuts, in the blender until smooth.

6. Pour mixture into saucepan and cook over medium-high heat, stirring constantly until thickened.

7. Add coconut and walnuts and stir to mix.

8. Allow to cool before spreading on cake.

MAKES 16 SERVINGS

PER 2" X 2" PIECE	
CALORIES	430
PROTEIN	6 g
CARBOHYDRATES	40 g
FIBER	7.5 g
FAT	28.5 g
SODIUM	135 mg

"Whether you eat or drink, or whatever you do, do all to the glory of God." — 1 CORINTHIANS 10:31, NKJV

Tofu Cheesecake

Light and beautiful, this cheesecake makes for a wonderful ending to any meal. Serve with **Strawberry Jam,** *page 113*, or **Berry Fruit Sauce,** *page 112*.

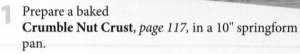

INGREDIENTS

20-oz can		crushed pineapple, in juice
3½	tbsp	cornstarch
½	cup	rinsed, raw cashews
2	12.3-oz	packages silken tofu, extra firm
½	cup	pineapple juice concentrate
⅓	cup	honey
½ rind		lemon *or*
½ tsp		lemon extract
½	tsp	salt

PER SERVING	
CALORIES	185
PROTEIN	8 g
CARBOHYDRATES	21 g
FIBER	1 g
FAT	8 g
SODIUM	100 mg

STEPS

1. Prepare a baked **Crumble Nut Crust,** *page 117,* in a 10" springform pan.

2. Combine crushed pineapple, cornstarch, and cashews in blender and blend smooth.

3. Add remaining ingredients and blend again.

4. Pour into springform pan with prepared crust.

5. Bake at 350°F for 45 minutes, cool and chill.

SERVINGS

COOK'S TIP

Fresh fanned strawberries are a beautiful garnish for this dessert. Make ⅛-inch-thick cuts toward the cap of the strawberry, then fan open.

"Have you found honey? Eat only as much as you need." — PROVERBS 25:16, NKJV

Vegan Tiramisu

Yes, there are a lot of steps to this version of the exquisite Italian dessert, but they are steps you will be glad you took!

INGREDIENTS

ESPRESSO SYRUP:

2½	tbsp	powdered coffee substitute (Roma)
1½	tbsp	carob powder
3	tbsp	water
1½	tbsp	maple syrup
1½	tsp	vanilla extract
2	dashes	salt

CUSTARD:

12.3	ounces	silken tofu, extra firm
2		13.5-oz cans coconut milk
¼	cup	turbinado sugar
½	tsp	stevia powder
⅛	tsp	salt
2	tsp	vanilla extract
1	tsp	**Espresso Syrup**
2	tbsp	Instant Clear Jel *or* cornstarch

CAKE:

½	cup	whole-wheat pastry flour
½	cup	unbleached flour
2	tsp	Ener-G baking powder *or*
1	tsp	Rumford baking powder
½	tsp	salt
3	tbsp	turbinado sugar
½	tsp	stevia powder
⅓	cup	white grape juice concentrate
⅓	cup	water
1	tsp	vanilla extract
3	tbsp	light olive oil

PER SERVING	
CALORIES	210
PROTEIN	3.5 g
CARBOHYDRATES	20 g
FIBER	1 g
FAT	13.5 g
SODIUM	105 mg

> **COOK'S TIP**
>
> In cake and custard, stevia powder can be replaced with ⅓ tablespoons more turbinado sugar. Also, Vegan Tiramisu can be assembled in two layers in an 8" x 8" pan.

STEPS

ESPRESSO SYRUP:

1. Combine all ingredients in a small saucepan and bring to boil. Allow to boil for 30 seconds. Cool.

CUSTARD:

1. Place all ingredients, except the Instant Clear Jel or cornstarch, in the blender and liquefy.

2. If using cornstarch, pour ½ cup of the blended mixture into a small bowl. Add the cornstarch and stir to mix well.

3. Heat the remaining custard in a large saucepan, stirring occasionally. When it begins to steam, add the cornstarch mixture and stir continually until it thickens. Allow to cool.

4. If using Instant Clear Jel, sprinkle it into the custard mixture gradually while the blended mixture is moving on medium speed.

5. Refrigerate the custard for 45 minutes to chill and thicken.

CAKE:

1. Preheat oven to 350°F.

2. Combine flours, baking powder, sugar, stevia powder, and salt in medium bowl and stir with a whisk to mix.

3. Combine juice concentrate, water, vanilla, and oil in another bowl and mix well.

4. Pour liquid mixture over dry ingredients and stir to mix, being careful not to stir bubbles out if using Ener-G baking powder.

5. Spread batter into an oil-sprayed 9" x 13" pan. The layer will be quite thin. Bake for 20 minutes.

6. After the cake has cooled, cut it into four strips for ease of handling, and then remove them from the pan. Wash this pan so it will be ready to assemble the recipe.

TO ASSEMBLE:

1. Pour all but 2 tablespoons of the Espresso Syrup into the bottom of the 9" x 13" pan. Tilt the pan to coat the bottom. Place the cake strips back into the pan.

2. Drizzle or brush the remaining Espresso Syrup on the cake. Place 2 tablespoons of carob powder in a tea strainer and dust the top of the cake.

3. Pour the chilled custard over the cake and refrigerate for about 30 minutes, until it begins to set.

4. Liberally dust the top of the Vegan Tiramisu with more of the carob powder. Place in refrigerator and continue to chill until firm.

MAKES 15 SERVINGS

Carob Fudge Sauce

Roma is an instant grain beverage that tastes much like coffee. Adding it to this recipe makes the fudge sauce taste much like its look-alike, the much-loved chocolate sauce. You'll be amazed.

INGREDIENTS

3	tbsp	carob powder
¾	cup	water
½	cup	dates
1	tbsp	peanut *or* almond butter
1	tsp	vanilla extract
⅛	tsp	salt
1	tsp	powdered coffee substitute (Roma)

PER 2 TABLESPOONS	
CALORIES	40
PROTEIN	.5 g
CARBOHYDRATES	9 g
FIBER	1 g
FAT	1 g
SODIUM	35 mg

STEPS

1 Heat carob powder, water, and dates until dates are soft and carob mixture is glossy.

2 Combine this mixture with remaining ingredients in the blender and blend until smooth.

3 Store in refrigerator. Freezes well.

MAKES 1½ CUPS

Variation: For **Carob Mint Sauce,** add ⅛ teaspoon peppermint extract. For **Carob Fudge Frosting,** decrease water to ½ cup.

Berry Fruit Sauce

On **Tofu Cheesecake,** *page 110,* **Belgian Waffles,** *page 51,* or **French Toast,** *page 50,* this sauce is beautiful and absolutely delicious.

INGREDIENTS

12-oz can		white grape raspberry juice concentrate
1	can	water
4	tbsp	cornstarch
1	16-oz package	frozen mixed berries, raspberries, *or* blueberries

PER ¼ CUP	
CALORIES	40
PROTEIN	.2 g
CARBOHYDRATES	9 g
FIBER	.5 g
FAT	0 g
SODIUM	2 mg

COOK'S TIP

Any flavor of juice concentrate can be used. Fresh fruit can also be used, of course. You might even want to try: white grape peach juice with frozen or fresh peaches, white grape cranberry with fresh sliced strawberries.

STEPS

1 Dissolve cornstarch in ½ cup of the water.

2 Heat juice and remaining water in saucepan until boiling.

3 Add cornstarch mixture and stir over medium-high heat until thickened.

4 Add frozen fruit, stir, and remove from heat.

MAKES 20 SERVINGS

"I give you every seed-bearing plant on the face of the whole earth and every tree that has fruit with seed in it. They will be yours for food." —GENESIS 1:29, NIV.

Strawberry Jam

An excellent breakfast spread or topping for **Tofu Cheesecake,** *page 110,* garnished with fresh sliced strawberries. Easy to whip up, this topping can be enjoyed year-round, as frozen berries work well.

INGREDIENTS

2½	cups	fresh *or* frozen strawberries
½	cup	pitted dates *or* dried pineapple

PER 2 TABLESPOONS	
CALORIES	60
PROTEIN	1 g
CARBOHYDRATES	16 g
FIBER	2.5 g
FAT	0 g
SODIUM	0 mg

STEPS

1. Thaw strawberries if frozen. Purée the berries in a blender.
2. If dates are not soft, place in small amount of water and steam in the microwave or on the stove.
3. Combine with strawberries in the blender and blend smooth. Chill to thicken. Keep refrigerated.

MAKES 1½ CUPS

Lemon Glaze

The perfect topping for the **Frozen Lemon Custard,** *page 121.* Simple and delicious.

INGREDIENTS

½	cup	pineapple juice
½	cup	water
3	tbsp	lemon juice
3	tbsp	turbinado sugar
1	tbsp	cornstarch

PER 2 TABLESPOONS	
CALORIES	25
PROTEIN	.1 g
CARBOHYDRATES	6.5 g
FIBER	0 g
FAT	0 g
SODIUM	2 mg

STEPS

1. Bring the pineapple juice and water to a boil in a small saucepan. Add sugar and stir with a whisk to dissolve.
2. Mix lemon juice and cornstarch in a small bowl. Add to boiling liquid and stir until thickened.
3. Cool slightly before serving.

MAKES 1¼ CUPS

Coconut Whipped Cream

Absolutely the best vegan whipped cream yet! Be sure to make this at least several hours ahead of time, then fluff with a whisk to produce a light and creamy whipped cream.

INGREDIENTS

13.5-oz can		coconut milk
½ 12.3-oz package		silken tofu, extra firm
2½	tbsp	turbinado sugar
1	tsp	vanilla extract
3	dashes	salt
2	tsp	Instant Clear Jel

PER 2 TABLESPOONS	
CALORIES	80
PROTEIN	1.5 g
CARBOHYDRATES	4 g
FIBER	0 g
FAT	7 g
SODIUM	55 mg

STEPS

1. Blend first four ingredients until smooth in blender, then while still blending, sprinkle in Instant Clear Jel.
2. Chill to thicken. Stir briefly before serving.

MAKES 12 SERVINGS

Carob Pudding

Few desserts are as delicious and healthy as this one. Garnish with a few nuts or granola on top for a little crunch or layer in a parfait glass with whipped topping for a beautiful presentation.

INGREDIENTS

¾	cup	hot water
½	cup	dates
2	tbsp	carob powder
1	tbsp	peanut butter
2	tsp	powdered coffee substitute (Roma)
⅛	tsp	salt
½	tsp	vanilla
1	cup	hot cooked millet
1	tbsp	coconut

STEPS

1. Soften dates by heating them together with the water.
2. Add remaining ingredients and blend smooth.
3. Serve warm or chilled.

MAKES 4 SERVINGS

PER SERVING	
CALORIES	185
PROTEIN	3.5 g
CARBOHYDRATES	35 g
FIBER	3 g
FAT	4.5 g
SODIUM	100 mg

Carob Mocha Mousse

Smooth and creamy goodness.

INGREDIENTS

13.5-oz can	coconut milk
12.3 ounces	firm, silken tofu
2 tbsp	honey
¼ cup	soft pitted dates
½ tsp	vanilla extract
1 tbsp	carob powder
1½ tsp	powdered coffee substitute (Roma)
2 dashes	salt
2 tsp	Instant Clear Jel

STEPS

1. Mix all ingredients, except Instant Clear Jel, in a blender until smooth.
2. Sprinkle in Instant Clear Jel while blender is running.
3. Pour into individual serving dishes, chill, and serve.

MAKES 8 SERVINGS

PER ½ CUP	
CALORIES	165
PROTEIN	5.5 g
CARBOHYDRATES	12 g
FIBER	1 g
FAT	12 g
SODIUM	65 mg

"Through the right exercise of the will, an entire change may be made in the lifestyle." — JOHN SCHARFFENBERG, M.D.

Zinia's Rice Pudding

This authentic Spanish-style rice pudding involves a few steps, but it achieves a delicate texture and subtle vanilla flavor. View the **StepFast Lifestyle Series,** program 11 video, for step-by-step Spanish cuisine instructions.

INGREDIENTS

1	cup	short grain brown rice
3	cups	soy *or* nut milk
1	cup	coconut milk
½	tsp	salt
⅓	cup	turbinado sugar
1	tsp	maple syrup
⅓	cup	raisins
1½	tsp	vanilla

PER ½ CUP	
CALORIES	190
PROTEIN	5 g
CARBOHYDRATES	29 g
FIBER	2 g
FAT	7 g
SODIUM	130 mg

STEPS

1. Wash and soak the short grain brown rice in hot water for about ½ hour while you assemble the other ingredients.

2. Drain rice and put it in a mini-food processor and cut it to resemble couscous or millet.

3. Cook the rice with the 3 cups of milk, the coconut milk, and salt for 20 minutes on medium heat. Creamy pudding needs slow, gentle cooking so the rice is tender and the milk is reduced.

4. After the rice is cooked, remove from heat and add the remaining ingredients. The pudding might be a little soupy, but it will thicken as it cools.

MAKES 10 SERVINGS

Flaky Piecrust

The lemon juice adds no tartness but contributes to a flaky texture.

INGREDIENTS

1⅛	cups	whole-wheat pastry flour
⅓	cup	unbleached flour
¼	tsp	salt
¼	cup	light olive oil
¼	cup	water
1	tsp	lemon juice

PER ⅛ RECIPE	
CALORIES	130
PROTEIN	9 g
CARBOHYDRATES	16 g
FIBER	2 g
FAT	6 g
SODIUM	75 mg

STEPS

1. Mix the flours and the salt in a medium bowl. Add remaining ingredients at the same time and stir until well mixed.

2. With your hands, press into a small ball. Place ball between two sheets of waxed paper. Dampen the tabletop to prevent the dough from slipping and roll it out.

3. Roll the ball out into a 10-inch circle. Remove the top sheet of waxed paper and place the crust in a 9-inch pie plate.

4. Bake at 350°F for 20 minutes for a baked pie shell or fill with filling and bake according to recipe.

MAKES 1 PIE CRUST

"Listen diligently to Me, and eat what is good, and let your soul delight itself in abundance." —ISAIAH 55:2, NKJV

Lemon Custard Pie

Rich and creamy, for very special occasions with a light meal.

INGREDIENTS

20-oz can	sliced pineapple, drained
½ tbsp	fresh lemon rind
13.5-oz can	coconut milk
¼ tsp	salt, slightly heaping
⅓ cup	honey
4½ tbsp	cornstarch
4 tbsp	fresh lemon juice
1/16 tsp	turmeric
1	piecrust

STEPS

1 In blender, blend all filling ingredients until smooth.

2 Cook mixture in a saucepan over medium heat until thick. Pour into a baked pie shell and chill until set.

MAKES 8 SERVINGS

PER SLICE	
CALORIES	300
PROTEIN	4 g
CARBOHYDRATES	32 g
FIBER	3.5 g
FAT	14 g
SODIUM	200 mg

Frozen Carob Mousse Pie

The texture is firm, but creamy and the flavor is wonderfully rich. Keep one of these in the freezer for unexpected guests.

INGREDIENTS

1½ 12.3 oz	packages firm, silken tofu
¼ cup	soymilk
¾ cup	carob chips
1 cup	pitted dates
⅓ cup	almond butter
½ tsp	salt (scant)
1½ tsp	vanilla extract
1½ tsp	powdered coffee substitute (Roma)
1	baked pie shell

STEPS

1 In a saucepan, heat first 4 ingredients until chips are melted.

2 Blend in blender with remaining ingredients until smooth and pour into baked pie shell.

3 Freeze until firm. Serve with **Coconut Whipped Cream,** *page 113*, and toasted pecans.

MAKES 10 SERVINGS

PER SLICE	
CALORIES	330
PROTEIN	10 g
CARBOHYDRATES	26 g
FIBER	5 g
FAT	15 g
SODIUM	600 mg

HEALTH TIP

Tofu is rich in high-quality protein and is a good source of B vitamins and iron. One-fourth pound of tofu contains 40 milligrams of healthy isoflavones, has almost no saturated fat, and, of course, has no cholesterol.

Blackberry Cobbler

COOK'S TIP
3 tablespoons turbinado sugar can be substituted for the stevia.

My mother was known for her Southern charm and hospitality, and she loved the arrival of summer when she could make a blackberry "roll." What she meant was blackberry cobbler. By any name, it's a yummy summertime favorite that can be served year-round since frozen blackberries are always available. But half the fun is picking the wild blackberries, which are organic and free, so if possible, midsummer, head for the berry patch!

INGREDIENTS

CRUST:

2¼	cups	whole-wheat pastry flour
¾	cup	unbleached flour
¾	tsp	salt
½	cup	light olive oil
½ cup + 1	tbsp	cold water
2	tsp	lemon juice

FILLING:

7	cups	blackberries, fresh *or* frozen
⅓	cup	white grape raspberry juice concentrate
2	tbsp	instant tapioca
½	tsp	stevia powder
1	tbsp	light olive oil
2	dashes	salt

STEPS

1. Mix the flours and the salt in a medium bowl. Add the remaining ingredients and stir until well mixed. With your hands, press in a smooth ball.

2. Divide the ball of dough in two and form two balls. Place one ball of dough between two sheets of waxed paper. Dampen the tabletop to prevent the dough from slipping as you roll it out.

3. Roll the first ball into a 10-inch circle. Remove the top sheet of waxed paper. Place the crust in an oil-sprayed 9-inch deep dish pie plate.

4. Fill with the blackberries, which have been mixed well with the other filling ingredients.

5. Roll out the top crust and place over the filling. Trim with scissors leaving ½ inch beyond the pie plate. Pinch the top and bottom crusts together along the edge. Cut 5 vents in the top crust with a sharp knife and decorate with leaves cut from the extra dough.

6. Bake at 350°F for 1 hour. Serve warm with **Vanilla Ice Cream,** *page 122.*

MAKES 10 SERVINGS

PER ⅒ PIE CRUST	
CALORIES	90
PROTEIN	3 g
CARBOHYDRATES	3 g
FIBER	2 g
FAT	3 g
SODIUM	440 mg

Crumble Nut Crust

Gluten-free goodness!

INGREDIENTS

½	cup	unsweetened coconut
½	cup	raw almonds
½	cup	brown rice flour
½	tsp	salt (scant)
2	tbsp	honey
2	tbsp	water

STEPS

1. Place coconut, almonds, flour, and salt in food processor. Blend together for about 30 seconds.

2. Add honey and process about 15 seconds more. Add water and blend again.

3. Press into a lightly oiled 9-inch pie plate, shaping with fingers to make a nicely formed piecrust.

4. Bake at 375°F for 10 minutes.

MAKES 1 PIECRUST

PER ⅛ PIE CRUST	
CALORIES	210
PROTEIN	4 g
CARBOHYDRATES	19.5 g
FIBER	3.9 g
FAT	4 g
SODIUM	110 mg

Lemon Pineapple Pie

The first vegetarian cookbook I ever used was Joann Rachor's **Of These Ye May Freely Eat.** It's full of many great recipes, including this one. Thanks, ladies!

INGREDIENTS

½	cup	rinsed, raw cashews
3	tbsp	lemon juice
2	tbsp	honey
1	tsp	vanilla
½	cup	water
¼	tsp	salt
⅓	cup	cornstarch
2½	cups	pineapple juice
¼	tsp	lemon extract *or*
1	tsp	lemon rind
¾	cup	crushed pineapple, in juice

STEPS

1. Pour 2 cups of the pineapple juice into a saucepan. Bring to a boil.

2. While juice is heating, combine all remaining ingredients, except the crushed pineapple, in the blender and blend smooth.

3. Add the blended mixture to the boiling juice and then cook and stir until thickened. Stir in well-drained pineapple.

4. Pour into prepared pie shell and chill or serve in custard dishes.

MAKES 8 SERVINGS

COOK'S TIP

Serve with a whipped topping. Pie can also be garnished with coconut, mandarin oranges and/or kiwi. If served as a pudding, top with Grape-Nuts or granola.

PER ⅛ PIE	
CALORIES	175
PROTEIN	3 g
CARBOHYDRATES	28 g
FIBER	1 g
FAT	6.5 g
SODIUM	75 mg

Pecan Pie

Pecan pie was my mother's calling card. Every new family in the neighborhood, the parents of every new baby, and those gathering for our family reunions had the privilege of enjoying some of her pecan pie. And I am happy to inform you that with a bright and beautiful smile on her face, Mama put her stamp of approval on this vegan version.

INGREDIENTS

1½	cups	water
6	tbsp	flaxseed
1⅓	cups	maple syrup
1½	cups	pitted dates
1	tsp	vanilla extract
1	tsp	maple extract
1	tsp	salt
½	cup	water (additional)
5	tbsp	cornstarch
2	cups	pecans, coarsely broken
3	tbsp	maple syrup (additional)
1		**Flaky Piecrust,** *page 115*

STEPS

1. Combine water and flaxseed in saucepan. Bring to a boil and continue boiling and stirring until thick, about 5 minutes. Pour into blender and blend until smooth.

2. Add the maple syrup, dates, extracts, salt, additional ½ cup of water, and the cornstarch to the flaxseed mixture and blend until smooth.

3. Toast pecans in a 300°F oven for 10 minutes.

4. Place pecans into a separate bowl and pour maple syrup and a sprinkle of salt over them. Stir to coat well. Reserve to place on top of filling.

5. Preheat oven to 350°F. Partially bake a 9-inch pie shell, about 8 minutes.

6. Pour filling into the pie shell. Bake for 15 minutes.

7. Remove from oven and gently arrange coated pecans on top of filling, pressing slightly into filling.

8. Bake for 20 more minutes or until set. Cool before serving. Serve at room temperature with **Vanilla Ice Cream,** *page 122.*

MAKES 12 SERVINGS

PER ⅛ PIE	
CALORIES	175
PROTEIN	3 g
CARBOHYDRATES	28 g
FIBER	1 g
FAT	7 g
SODIUM	75 mg

COOK'S TIP

This pie has healthful ingredients, but it is also very rich. Serve small servings on a special occasion with a menu that is low in fat.

Strawberry Sorbet

Delightfully smooth and creamy.

INGREDIENTS

6	small	frozen bananas, sliced (3 cups)
1½	cups	frozen strawberries
½	cup	dairy-free milk powder
	pinch	salt
¼	cup	white grape raspberry frozen juice concentrate

STEPS

1. Slightly thaw the bananas and strawberries.
2. Blend all the ingredients in a food processor or blender.
3. Pour into a container and freeze.
4. Slightly thaw and serve with an ice-cream scoop.

MAKES 10 SERVINGS

PER ½ CUP	
CALORIES	70
PROTEIN	2 g
CARBOHYDRATES	15.5 g
FIBER	2 g
FAT	1 g
SODIUM	10 mg

Variation: Substitute peaches for strawberries and add ½ teaspoon of almond extract for **Peach Sorbet.**

Orange Crush

A happy ending to a hot, summer day.

INGREDIENTS

½	cup	orange juice concentrate
½		frozen banana
2	cups	soymilk
1	tsp	vanilla extract
	dash	salt
12		ice cubes

STEPS

1. Cut the banana into chunks.
2. In a blender, blend smooth all ingredients except the ice.
3. Gradually add ice as you blend, until thick.
4. Garnish with fresh orange slices.

MAKES 2 SERVINGS

PER SERVING	
CALORIES	265
PROTEIN	11 g
CARBOHYDRATES	45.5 g
FIBER	4.5 g
FAT	5 g
SODIUM	110 mg

Frozen Lemon Custard

These individual desserts can be made ahead to give the royal treatment to even unexpected guests, who will never guess they are eating tofu!

INGREDIENTS

12.3 ounces	firm, silken tofu
¼ cup	lemon juice
3 tbsp	honey
3 tbsp	light olive oil
¹⁄₁₆ tsp	salt
1 tsp	fresh lemon rind
dash	turmeric
⅓ cup	chopped nuts

STEPS

1. Place all ingredients, except nuts, in a blender and blend until smooth.

2. Line muffin tin with eight paper muffin cups. Sprinkle chopped nuts into the bottom of each muffin cup and pour tofu mixture into the cups.

3. Place in freezer for several hours or until set.

4. Serve with **Lemon Glaze**, *page 113*, **Carob Fudge Sauce**, *page 112*, or **Berry Fruit Sauce**, *page 112*.

MAKES 8 SERVINGS

PER SERVING	
CALORIES	165
PROTEIN	8 g
CARBOHYDRATES	9 g
FIBER	1.5 g
FAT	12 g
SODIUM	25 mg

Piña Colada

Asian paper umbrellas make this a fun supper drink that you can eat with a spoon.

INGREDIENTS

1 cup	pineapple juice
½ cup	coconut milk
2	frozen bananas
¼ tsp	coconut extract

STEPS

1. Slice bananas into chunks, combine with remaining ingredients in a blender, and blend smooth.

2. Add more or fewer banana chunks according to desired consistency.

3. For firmer consistency, place thick mixture directly into freezer and freeze for 30 to 60 minutes.

MAKES 2 SERVINGS

PER SERVING	
CALORIES	250
PROTEIN	3 g
CARBOHYDRATES	46 g
FIBER	3.5 g
FAT	9 g
SODIUM	3 mg

HEALTH TIP

Adults should consume about 4,500 milligrams of potassium each day. We all know that bananas are an excellent source of potassium. A medium banana contains 450 milligrams, but a medium baked potato provides 800 milligrams.

Vanilla Ice Cream

Delicious with fresh peaches or **Carob Fudge Sauce,** *page 112!*

INGREDIENTS

1	cup	raw almonds
1	can	coconut milk
⅓	cup	honey
2	tsp	vanilla
½	tsp	stevia powder
¼	tsp	salt
5	cups	ice cubes

PER ½ CUP SERVING	
CALORIES	160
PROTEIN	3.5 g
CARBOHYDRATES	11 g
FIBER	1 g
FAT	12 g
SODIUM	55 mg

STEPS

1. Blend all ingredients in blender until smooth.
2. Gradually add 5 cups of ice cubes, blending until smooth and thick.
3. Serve immediately for "soft serve" texture. Pour into container and freeze 2 to 3 hours for firmer consistency. If completely frozen, allow to thaw at room temperature for about 30 minutes.

MAKES 6 CUPS

Old-fashioned Ice Cream

With this old-fashioned ice cream, you can make any flavor. If you have a hand-crank ice-cream freezer, that's all the better. Everyone can get some exercise while the excitement mounts!

INGREDIENTS

3	13.5-oz cans coconut milk	
3	cans	vanilla Silk soymilk
¾	cup	turbinado sugar
1	tbsp	vanilla extract
¼	tsp	salt
2	tbsp	light olive oil

PER ½ CUP	
CALORIES	170
PROTEIN	39 g
CARBOHYDRATES	12 g
FIBER	.5 g
FAT	13 g
SODIUM	4 mg

STEPS

1. Blend all ingredients in blender to dissolve sugar.
2. Pour into an ice-cream freezer. Freeze as with conventional ice-cream recipe, using ice and rock salt, for about 45 minutes.

MAKES 22 SERVINGS

Variation: To make **Peach Ice Cream,** freeze the custard, then add 1 cup diced fresh peaches and 1 teaspoon almond extract, mix well, and place ice cream in the freezer.

COOK'S TIP

An alternate method of freezing is to pour into ice trays and freeze. Then run the cubes though a Champion juicer, or thaw slightly and purée in a blender with a small amount of soymilk.

Strawberry Smoothie

This classic smoothie can be made with fruits of your choice. The bananas give it the smooth, creamy texture, and the berries or tropical fruits, such as mango or kiwi, will give it color and distinctive flavor.

INGREDIENTS

1	cup	pineapple juice
2		frozen bananas
8	large	frozen strawberries, slightly thawed

PER SERVING	
CALORIES	90
PROTEIN	1 g
CARBOHYDRATES	23 g
FIBER	2 g
FAT	.2 g
SODIUM	2 mg

STEPS

1. Slice frozen bananas into ½-inch slices and place them in a blender.

2. Add pineapple juice and strawberries, then blend all ingredients into a thick shake.

3. Garnish each serving with granola, if desired.

MAKES 4 SERVINGS

COOK'S TIP

To freeze bananas, peel ripe bananas, place into a plastic bag, and freeze. I like to slice them before freezing them so I can skip that step when making frozen treats.

"A cheerful heart is good medicine." —PROVERBS 17:22, NIV

Index